PRAISE FOR
INTERNATIONAL S̶U̶P̶P̶L̶Y̶
CHAIN RELATIONSHIPS

'Patrick eloquently captures the reality that the modern world is a highly connected place that operates as an integrated system, and the associated trade-related causes and effects. He offers some interesting food for thought in a world where increasingly the politics of national self-interest are usurping the politics of mutual interest, and challenges some of the misconceptions of globalization.'
Kevin Martin, Global Procurement Director, Pharmaceuticals/FMCG

'International supply chain relationships are in flux, with the rise of nationalistic sentiment and looming trade wars. It is critical that professionals who understand and appreciate the economic and social benefits of global supply chain relationships champion their evolution. This book is a very valuable contribution to this complex topic. Few possess Patrick's deep understanding of international supply chains, from the basic nuts and bolts of how supply chains function to the global strategies that enable them. This book is very timely, and a must read for all engaged or interested in international supply chain relationships.'
Joseph Heffernan, Head of Production and Materials Planning, Merck Group

'We tend to acknowledge globalization and inter-connectedness, but when asked for details describe some kind of Rubik's cube. In this intriguing book, Patrick Daly provides the clear, pragmatic reality of international supply chains and how to create and exploit them towards greater profit and success. Forget the puzzle and listen to the expert.'
Alan Weiss, author of *Million Dollar Consulting* and over 50 other books in 15 languages, Rhode Island, USA

'Patrick Daly has proved his expertise on many occasions and his advice has always been of great help in everything related to logistics, regardless of whether the interested party was a large corporation or a SME. In this book, Patrick puts his expertise and experience within reach of anyone who needs to improve the value chain of their products and services. He provides a clear view of the opportunities that are available to all anywhere in the world. Thank you, Patrick, for shining some light into the deep, dark world of globalization.'

Miguel Díaz Abella, Director General, Zalia, Spain (retired)

'Occasionally a book comes along from someone who is seasoned in providing truly successful, hands-on solutions that we can learn from. Patrick has three decades of successful project completion on several continents, including for my own previous employer, Procter & Gamble. His learning has been gleaned from those experiences and is reflected all through this book. It is my pleasure to recommend this excellent publication.'

Liam Cassidy, Managing Director, LCL Consult Ltd, Dublin and Shanghai

'Patrick Daly has written an understandable roadmap for business people working to navigate the complexities of globalization and international supply chains. It simplifies, but is in no way simplistic. Read this book – and learn from one of the best.'

Rebecca Morgan, President, Fulcrum ConsultingWorks Inc, Cleveland OH, USA

'The outcome of the 2016 UK Brexit referendum sent shockwaves throughout the Irish manufacturing sector, but particularly through Small and Medium Enterprises (SMEs) focussed on a single market. As sterling plunged, the certainties of making a living out of the British market evaporated to be replaced by the anxieties of building business further afield. For anyone facing into these challenges, Patrick Daly's new book is invaluable. Not only is it an easy read that encourages SME exporters to try harder and smarter, but it also alerts them to the threats to their own business from firms previously not interested in their local market. In a rapidly changing world of new trade deals, IT and logistics platforms, this book could run to several editions.'

Howard Knott, MA, FCILT Logistics consultant to the Irish Exporters Association and columnist for *Fleet Transport*

'A thoroughly readable book, in which the language and the content are very clear. It is a book that should be read by all who want to develop their business in a direction that will yield profits securely into the future. I will recommend *International Supply Chain Relationships* to my clients, colleagues and any other business people.'

Malachi Spain, career and business owner advisor, Malachi Spain Ltd, Dublin, Ireland

To Tim,
With compliments.
05. 05. 22

International Supply Chain Relationships

Creating competitive advantage in a globalized economy

Patrick Daly

First published in Great Britain and the United States in 2019 by Kogan Page Limited

2nd Floor, 45 Gee Street	c/o Martin P Hill Consulting	4737/23 Ansari Road
London	122 W 27th St, 10th Floor	Daryaganj
EC1V 3RS	New York, NY 10001	New Delhi 110002
United Kingdom	USA	India
www.koganpage.com		

© Patrick Daly, 2019

ISBNs

Hardback	978 0 7494 9780 4
Paperback	978 0 7494 8003 5
eBook	978 0 7494 8004 2

British Library Cataloguing-in-Publication Data

A CIP record for this book is available from the British Library.

Library of Congress Cataloging-in-Publication Data

Names: Daly, Patrick (Writer on international economics) author.
Title: International supply chain relationships : creating competitive
    advantage in a globalized economy / Patrick Daly.
Description: 1 Edition. | New York : Kogan Pgae Ltd, [2019] | Includes
    bibliographical references.
Identifiers: LCCN 2018052625 (print) | LCCN 2019000299 (ebook) | ISBN
    9780749480042 (ebook) | ISBN 9780749480035 (pbk. : alk. paper) | ISBN
    9780749497804 (hardback : alk. paper) | ISBN 9780749480042 (eISBN)
Subjects: LCSH: Business logistics. | International economic relations. |
    Communication–International cooperation.
Classification: LCC HD38.5 (ebook) | LCC HD38.5 .D35 2019 (print) | DDC
    658.7–dc23
LC record available at https://lccn.loc.gov/2018052625

Typeset by Integra Software Services, Pondicherry
Print production managed by Jellyfish
Printed and bound by CPI Group (UK) Ltd, Croydon CR0 4YY

To Elisa, Brian and Maria
A vosotros, siempre.

CONTENTS

ABOUT THE AUTHOR

Patrick Daly is the founder and Managing Director of Alba Consulting, a business consultancy focused on supply chain and logistics based in Dublin, Ireland. Patrick is an accomplished consultant, speaker, trainer, author and broadcaster and has been active in the logistics sector for over 25 years.

Patrick works with many of the top Fortune 500 companies in manufacturing, distribution and logistics services in Europe, Asia and the Americas, helping them to achieve dramatic improvements in their supply chain capabilities and performance through supply chain excellence. In his consultancy assignments, Patrick has worked with clients all over the world in countries such as China, India, Uruguay, Puerto Rico, Egypt, UAE, US, UK, Spain, Croatia and others.

Patrick is the chairman of the Irish Exporters Association supply chain series and former president of the association's Latin America Trade Forum. Patricks hosts Interlinks, a weekly radio programme broadcast on Dublin South FM that explores the positive and negative effects of globalization around the world through the medium of interviews with business people from around the world.

Patrick is married with two children and lives in Dublin, Ireland. He is a fluent speaker of Spanish, having lived in Spain for 10 years and with his Spanish wife has raised a bilingual household. Patrick is an active sportsman who skis, runs and plays soccer and tag rugby and completed the Dublin marathon in 2011.

PREFACE

'We are all caught in an inescapable network of mutuality, tied in a single garment of destiny. Whatever affects one destiny, affects all indirectly.'

MARTIN LUTHER KING JR

We live in a globalized world we are being told incessantly on the newscasts. We hear about the globalized economy, the global marketplace, global culture and even the global war on terror. But what is globalization and what does it mean for you as an individual manager or business owner? Is it a threat or is it an opportunity and whatever it is, what should you do about it? Indeed, what *can* you do about it? The accelerating changes that we can all observe occurring in the day-to-day world of business, such as increased foreign competition in our home markets, global sourcing, exporting, offshoring, foreign direct investment and international recruitment are the manifestation of the effects of globalization that we are most familiar with in our businesses.

The causes that are driving these changes are broad and deep and have acquired a momentum that could only be stopped by a major world conflagration causing nations to close in upon themselves. These drivers are meta-trends and they include trade deregulation, advances in information and communications technology and the integration of transport modes and infrastructure. Consequently, businesses of all types and sizes, and not just multinational corporations, are having to respond urgently to these changes, if they wish to survive and thrive. The best among them are developing strategies, plans and techniques to mitigate the threats and to take advantage of the opportunities presented by this globalization of business. Many have looked to the ideas, tools and concepts of supply chain management (SCM) as a framework to help them make sense of the new degrees of complexity and connectedness that result from working in an economy with so many interconnected partners spread across very large geographical areas.

Supply chain management adopts a *systems approach* to analysing the interconnected networks that businesses now find themselves embedded within and is particularly suited to this purpose. However, much of the available literature is based on the challenges and experiences of very large corporations and consequently many managers and business owners of smaller- and medium-sized enterprises (SMEs) find these cases difficult to relate to their own situation. In this book I aim to provide the managers and owners of SMEs with a solid understanding of the thinking habits, hard and soft skills and worldview required to be successful in the highly interconnected business environment of the early 21st century. I argue that the crucial differentiator that will set apart the most successful firms will be the quality and strength of the connections that they build with the full panoply of partners in their supply chains. I explain how the tools and techniques of supply chain management can be translated and applied to the realities faced by SMEs as the effects of globalization continue to reach parts of the economy hitherto sheltered from the winds of change.

If you internalize the message within this book and apply the lessons encapsulated in its pages I am sure that you will discover untapped resources in yourself and in your business and develop the confidence to reach new horizons and set your business on a path of sustainable success for the future. As a bonus to you for buying this book and as an expression of my gratitude you can obtain some bonus content to help you on your way by visiting www.albalogistics.com/iscrbook and entering the code SCM4007.

I wish you the very best on this exciting journey.

Patrick Daly, Bray, Co Wicklow, Ireland

ACKNOWLEDGEMENTS

My gratitude to Dr Alan Weiss who made me believe that it was possible to write this book and was instrumental in the practical formulation of the proposal that led to the ultimate success of its acceptance by my publisher, Kogan Page.

My thanks to Joe Dalton of Breakthrough Brands, marketing genius, who has provided me with websites, blogs, videos, social media, promotion and the impetus to continue to build my business to new heights.

Special thanks also to Malachi Spain, a gentleman and a scholar, who always helps me to see things from a unique angle, sometimes by just holding up a mirror to me face figuratively speaking, and who has been a source or comfort and encouragement to me in my professional and personal life for over a decade.

My thanks, together with my sympathy, to the editors of my publisher Kogan Page, Julia Swales, Amy Minshull and Rajveer Ro'isin Singh, for their patience, critique, feedback and encouragement along the way while writing the chapters of *International Supply Chain Relationships*.

In memory of my friend John Dalton, long lost, re-found, and sadly passed, who taught me never to be afraid, no matter how scary the vista appears to be.

And most of all, thanks to my wonderful wife Elisa who has been with me through the many ups and downs of a marriage, the raising of a family and the running of a business for almost 30 years.

The globalization of business and the supply chain management concept

01

What is globalization?

Globalization is a term that we hear a lot in the media. Often the term comes with negative associations of job losses and falling wages in developed countries due to competition from abroad and the offshoring of business activities to developing markets in Asia, Latin America and Eastern Europe. There is an idea that globalization is new, that it is ubiquitous and that it is threatening. However, globalization is not a new phenomenon nor is it evenly spread in space or in time. Whether or not it constitutes a threat, or an opportunity, very much depends on where you are, how you earn your living and how you choose to respond to its effects. Globalization has ebbed and flowed in waves over the course of history. Just over one hundred years ago, before the outbreak of world war one, the world was in some ways even more globalized than it is today with people and capital enjoying quite a high degree of freedom to move and deploy from one part of the globe to another. The current wave of globalization that we are experiencing in the early 21st century is being wrought by three fundamental changes that are transforming the world economically, politically and socially.

Information and communications technology

Firstly, advances in information and communications technology manifested in cloud computing, the Global Positioning System (GPS), Radio Frequency Identification (RFID), and many other technologies have totally changed the speed and accuracy with which information is accessed, analysed and used to inform task accomplishment and decision-making, whether that be optimizing delivery routes, transmitting advance shipping notices for goods in transit, or enabling collaborative teams to work together across multiple time zones. Take for example Walmart, which pioneered the use of RFID technology in the early 2000s in its retail network to manage, control and optimize its vast inventories of products. After a slow start in penetrating the wider supply networks and a steep learning curve in the correct application of the technology, RFID tags and readers and other technologies such as NFR (Near Field Range) are now becoming ubiquitous in everything from retail, libraries and security to public transport, hospitals and healthcare.

Deregulation and liberalization

Secondly, the liberalization and deregulation of international trade and investment has opened opportunities for business expansion, diversification and innovation that were unimaginable a few short decades ago. International trade and foreign direct investment, despite a hiatus due to the Great Recession in 2008, have reached levels never seen before. According to the World Trade Organization (WTO) global trade in merchandise was approximately $15 trillion in 2014 and trade in services reached almost $5 trillion (WTO, 2017). Whereas international trade accounted for just 20 per cent of global GDP in 1995, this had risen to 30 per cent by 2015 and global trade now has a significant influence on global GDP. Likewise, the world stock of foreign direct investment reached a figure in excess of $26 trillion in 2014 according to the CIA World Fact Book. This trend is even affecting countries that previously were at the margins of international commerce. Take Cuba for example, a country long isolated from international trade and foreign investment due to ideology and embargos. In 2014 the Cuban legislature announced a new legal framework to attract foreign direct investment that includes the option of majority foreign ownership of enterprises in Cuba. On 31 March 2014 the Cuban Communist Party daily, *Granma*, quoted an official source as saying, 'no country today has successfully developed without foreign investment as a component of its political economy'.

No doubt we are currently living through a time where there are certain strains appearing within the global trading system with increases in tariffs and the looming threat of a trade war between the US, the EU and China. It is uncertain at this point how this will play out in the longer term and whether there will be a prolonged bout of protectionism that depresses world trade as occurred in the 1930s or whether the various posturing, threats and negotiations from the major global trading powers will lead to a reduction in tariffs and barriers. In any case, with trade now representing 30 per cent of global GDP and global supply chains having become so enmeshed and embedded in the modern economy, international trade, and particularly intra-regional trade will continue to be a significant feature of the world economy in the future (Ghemawat, 2018).

Transportation innovation

Thirdly, significant advances in the quality and reach of global transportation technology and the improvement and integration of transport networks are making trade and investment viable in parts of the world that had previously been inaccessible. The advent of purpose-built container ships in the mid-1950s and dedicated airfreight services from the 1980s revolutionized global logistics. Since then, ongoing investment in ports, airports, road, rail and intermodal transport hubs have given rise to global logistics hubs such as Memphis, Rotterdam and Singapore, which act as poles and nodes of economic development and market access in an integrated global network. One of the most significant transport infrastructure investments in the world was the Panama Canal expansion project, which completed in 2016 and doubles the capacity of the canal linking the Pacific Ocean and the Atlantic Ocean through the Caribbean Sea. The new Panamax size ships that are able to transit the canal have double the capacity of the previous Panamax vessels. Consequently, many east coast US ports as well as European ports are upgrading their facilities in order to cater for these new larger vessels. The canal is predicted to double its current merchandise throughput by 2025.

SMEs and globalization

All these transformations, which have gathered pace significantly over the last 30 years, are facilitating the rapid spread of the webs of supply and distribution of products and services all over the globe in an unprecedented fashion. Not only is this so for multinational corporations, but the transformations are also enabling, indeed in many cases forcing, small- and medium-sized enterprises (SMEs) out of local and national constraints and onto a global stage. This is having dramatic implications for all types and sizes of companies wherever they are in the world. For these SMEs to compete successfully on an international stage usually means dealing with multiple partners in order to produce and deliver consistently high-quality products and services at competitive prices to their customers across the world. These partners may include different combinations of suppliers of materials and services, transport carriers, logistics service providers, distributors, wholesalers, retailers, marketers, product designers, business consultants and others. To thrive in new and innovative ways, businesses need to purposefully configure strong and effective chains and networks with these multiple partners. This new complexity, particularly when it takes place across international borders, is giving rise to new risks and challenges for small- and medium-sized businesses all over the world.

Of course, the effects of globalization are not spread evenly across the globe and this has very important implications for businesses looking to develop effective strategies to enable them to compete and thrive in a globalized economy. Some parts of the world are far more integrated into the global trade, transport and communications networks than are others. Places such as Singapore, Memphis and Rotterdam are truly integrated and globalized business locations embedded into the transport, communications and trade networks, whereas others such as Kathmandu, Medellin and Ankara are aspiring global business centres while places like Timbuktu, Dushanbe and Pyongyang are, for the time being at least, well off the global beaten track.

Location still matters very much in the global economy when it comes to selecting which export markets to enter and where to establish overseas operations. The meta-trends that we have mentioned in communications technology, trade deregulation and transport have brought about a situation whereby businesses can no longer hope to simply operate and compete in the longer term at a local or even a national level except for those providing very personalized services that must be delivered in a local context such as haircuts or cups of coffee. Whereas in the past only the very large multinational corporations operated and competed transnationally, increasingly this is becoming a requirement for medium- and smaller-sized companies also. This is because competitors from other regions and countries can access and compete in the home markets of these smaller-sized businesses in ways that were not possible until quite recently and therefore if they do not equip themselves to compete internationally, they may have 'their lunch eaten' by foreign competitors in their own back yard.

By way of example, let's consider the live shellfish business in Spain. The Spanish are among the world's largest consumers of shellfish such as crab, lobster, crayfish and shrimp. The average Spaniard consumes nearly 100 lbs (42.4 kg) of fish and shellfish annually compared to about 50 lbs (23 kg) per person in the US and the UK (FAO, 2015). Typically, the Spanish buy their shellfish live in supermarkets, traditional fishmongers and restaurants. Much of the product is imported in temperature-controlled and oxygenated seawater tanks carried on heavy goods vehicles from Ireland, Scotland and Norway. Up until recent times, the distribution of live shellfish in Spain was dominated by local wholesale distributors who purchased from the suppliers in the supplier countries and maintained control over the retail market within Spain, delivering to them from stocks of live product held in so called 'vivier' installations close to the retail points of sale. However, in recent times, live shellfish suppliers from the northern European supplier countries with greater financial resources, a more international vision of business and mobile digital technology capability have begun to set up their own holding facilities and distribution capabilities within the target markets in Spain supplying directly to the end consumers with guarantees of supply, quality and cost unmatchable by the incumbents. This is deeply disruptive to the status quo. This is a sudden and unexpected challenge for the incumbent wholesalers in the Spanish national market who now face challenges from outside and who themselves will now be forced to innovate and diversify outside their traditional markets in order to survive. I have met personally with several who are moving into producing high-end pre-cooked seafood meals for export to other European countries and further afield.

What are the implications of globalization for your business?

This type of unforeseen, disruptive competition presents a set of startling new challenges to companies in developed economies all over the world, and particularly to those in the small- to mid-size range ($5 million to $100 million annual sales) operating in local and regional markets within their own countries and who may have felt safe from outside competition up to this point in time. Many of these companies have had little or no experience of doing business in international markets and it is becoming ever more unsustainable to operate a thriving business in this insular, inward-looking way. One of the three key drivers of the current wave of globalization that we have identified is the deregulation and liberalization of trade and overseas investment. This deregulation is continuing apace on many fronts with, for example, new free trade arrangements coming into force between the EU and Canada and the EU and Mexico as well as between those Asia-Pacific nations, excluding the US, that have decided to forge on with what was the TPP (Trans-Pacific Partnership). Therefore, trade deregulation and liberalization are still advancing despite the advance of protectionism and the raising of trade barriers on some fronts, together with opposition from non-governmental organizations (NGOs) and from the representatives of certain industrial sectors, and this is set to create a world in which, in the long run, international trade and investment will gain ever more importance in the global economy.

For example, on 5 October 2015 the US and 11 other Pacific Rim countries reached agreement on the TPP, a free trade agreement that will come into force after a two-year ratification process on the part of the participating countries. While the current US Administration later decided to opt out of the TPP, the remaining nations decided to forge ahead and there is some indication, at the time of writing, that the US may wish to re-join the arrangement at some point in the future. The stated aim of the TPP is to enhance trade and investment among the members through the elimination of tariffs, lower service barriers and the protection of the rights of foreign investors. This trade agreement whose signatories include Canada, Mexico, Peru, Chile, Australia, New Zealand, Japan, Vietnam, Brunei, Malaysia and Singapore means increased trade flows and competition within and among these countries with a total GDP of nearly $12 trillion (IMF, 2018). While the US and the EU in 2016 suspended indefinitely the process of negotiating a similar free trade agreement, the Transatlantic Trade and Investment Partnership (TTIP), to enhance trade and investment between the US and the 28 member states of the European Union, there were some indications by mid-2017 that negotiations might resume at some point in the future (Deutsche Welle, 2017). These two blocs together represent some 60 per cent of world GDP, a third of current global trade in merchandise and over two-fifths of world trade in services. At the time of writing, in mid-2018, the future of this agreement is very uncertain but if the US under a current or future administration re-engages with these agreements, world trade could increase significantly from current levels.

Threat or opportunity

These developments constitute both a threat and an opportunity for your business. The threat is that posed by competitors from other regions coming into your home markets under the protection of trade deregulation, and leveraging the capabilities of modern transport networks, information technology and digital communications to compete with you, gain market share and if you are not prepared, eat your lunch! On the other hand, the opportunity is that it has never been so viable for you to diversify your own business to access both suppliers and customers to improve your competitiveness, innovate and access new markets. This will enable you to grow while at the same time becoming more robust and more profitable; in short, to thrive. That is of course, provided you have the right strategy and provided you have the right skills and attributes in your team to take advantage of the opportunity to implement the strategy effectively. We have already seen the case of the Spanish live seafood wholesalers being challenged by innovative newcomers from other European Union member states. There are many other examples, such as that of the Irish airline Ryanair. In 2015, the company celebrated the 30th anniversary of its first scheduled service, which flew from Waterford, Ireland to London in England on 8 July 1985, with its sole aircraft, a 15-seater Embraer Bandierante turboprop (DublinAirport.com, 2015).

In 1985, the European aviation industry was highly regulated and restricted, with national flag-carrier airlines such as British Airways, Air France and Lufthansa dominating the scene. Deregulation of the European aviation industry in 1997 was the catalyst that allowed Ryanair to become the largest European airline by scheduled passengers carried. In 2015 the company was operating over 300 Boeing 737-800 aircraft, flying to 191 destinations, with projected revenues of more than €5.6 billion. Successful strategies require a willingness, capability and confidence to build multiple connections and relationships that are necessary to take advantage of the new possibilities and opportunities. The question to be answered is, how do you as a business owner or manager formulate and implement robust strategies that will allow your business to thrive in this new environment in which cooperation with a multitude of players spread over wide geographical areas is going to be critical for your survival and success as a business, particularly if this is a new and unfamiliar situation for your company.

One aspect of the capabilities that need to be developed and that may constitute a challenge for smaller- and medium-sized companies that are otherwise competent and disciplined in their area of business, is the acquisition and development of the key communication and cultural skills. These will be needed to interact successfully with partner companies and official authorities in other jurisdictions where business culture, social norms and language may be very different from what they are accustomed to in the home market. These can be daunting challenges for companies and can undermine confidence and the resolve to persevere to a successful outcome. Opening new foreign markets through the building of strong relationships with channel partners such as distributors or resellers, as well as progressing from exporting to investment by setting up wholly-owned, or joint-venture, distribution or manufacturing operations requires a level of knowledge and sophistication that encompasses the cultural, political, logistical and financial aspects of the target market. These are skills and competences that may be new and unfamiliar for companies that heretofore have only operated in local or national markets. Nonetheless, investment in these skills and competences will report manifold benefits to your business because they strengthen the links at the points where your business interfaces with supply chain partners.

The implication for many companies will be the need to incorporate and leverage diversity into their workforce. Once aspect of this is language skills. While English is undoubtedly the international business language and has been adopted as the sole language of operation by many multinational corporations, even some that do not have their home base in an English-speaking country, for smaller companies who must project themselves internationally through the strength of their relationships, the recruitment of individuals who are bilingual and multilingual into key positions will be a key factor for success in gaining a competitive advantage. These are skills that tend to be in short supply in many of the English-speaking countries. In Ireland for example, a country that depends hugely on international trade for its economic success, its Department of Education and Skills, in its consultation document on foreign language strategy states: 'people who are bilingual or multilingual tend to be more flexible, more creative and more fluent in their mother tongue. They communicate more clearly and accurately to diverse audiences and are much sought after by employers.'

The supply chain concept, sounds great in theory but...

Supply chain management (SCM) theory provides a framework for dealing with this new paradigm. Many of the world's top global organizations have internalized the tenets of SCM into their corporate DNA and have reached high levels of competence in the execution of effective supply chain strategies. Consequently, there are many publications and case studies that describe in detail how they have faced up to, and overcome, a wide range of challenges in the management of their global supply chains, from Dell's configure-to-order model for mass-customization of PCs, to the Toyota Production System based on the smoothing of production flow to eliminate waste, and Zara's consistently super-fast introduction of new fashion lines in small batches to maximize full-price sales of garments and apparel and minimize discounted sales. However, these examples and the publications in which they are described and discussed, along with much of the literature available on supply chain management theory are often of a scale, technicality and complexity to which the owners and managers of smaller- and medium-sized businesses often find it difficult to relate to their own circumstances and experiences. Therefore, the question that concerns us here is how can these concepts, principles and tools be learned, adapted and applied by small- and medium-sized businesses to enable them to benefit from what they have to offer. That is, how can small- and medium-sized businesses apply these principles in ways that are pragmatic, practical and lead to measurable business benefits?

Competence, discipline and confidence

As a prerequisite for success, three key qualities are required: competence, discipline and confidence. All three of these qualities are essential. Absent any one and you will not be able to fully leverage the presence of the other two. **Competence** refers to the business and technical know-how that you need to have to be able to conduct business in your chosen sector. Chances are, that if you have been successful in business so far, you possess a high degree of competence and expertise in your field related to product, market, sales or some other key element that is the key driving force of your business. **Discipline** refers to the processes, standardization and measurement that ensure consistency in quality and service. Again, if you have been successful in business up to this point you will have key financial, operational and organizational metrics in place that indicate how well you are progressing towards achieving your business objectives. **Confidence** arises from the set of cultural and interpersonal skills, knowledge and attributes that enable your organization to enter into, and successfully manage relationships with other organizations to work together both nationally and internationally to achieve common objectives that deliver competitive advantage. It is the skill set that is most often undervalued, underappreciated and overlooked, but the one that is most often the difference between mediocrity and excellence in my opinion.

If you didn't have the required competence and discipline to conduct business in your sector, you probably wouldn't be in business today. Consequently, among small- and medium-sized businesses, what is most often missing when it comes to leveraging the full potential of supply chain management is not the technical competence required to produce competitive goods and services, nor is it the discipline to manage and control the quality and performance of their business, but rather it is the confidence required to establish the effective, mutually beneficial business relationships, required to successfully conduct business internationally. Those businesses that possess or can acquire the skills and attributes that will underpin the confidence to enable them to build and sustain these crucial supply chain relationships that are required to grow, innovate and diversify will avoid the risk of being outmanoeuvred by aggressive outside players landing in their home market. Furthermore, they will be best equipped to venture forth outside their traditional markets, and areas of activity to forge value-added relationships in the crucible that is the interface between their organization and the multiple supply chain partners with whom they will work collaboratively to deliver their products and services to markets across the world. The ideal place to be in Figure 1.1 is the sweet spot in the middle where competence, discipline and confidence overlap.

Figure 1.1   The competence, confidence, discipline sweet spot

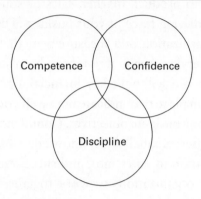

The systems approach

One of the standout and original features of supply chain management is that it adopts a *systems approach* to considering the complexity of the networks of supply, production and distribution that businesses develop to acquire and process the materials, technologies and information that they need to produce the goods and services that their customers require to satisfy their needs and wants. This systems approach has nothing to do with information technology systems, but rather it is about a way of thinking about complex business networks and relationships that is different from what is generally our default and habitual way of thinking. Rather than viewing things in isolation and in silos, the systems approach challenges us to think in terms of the whole network and how we can work with other players to improve its outputs for the benefit of all the stakeholders. This is relatively easy to grasp in theory but often very challenging to implement in practice.

Unfortunately, the metaphor of the chain when we think of supply chain management, is not a particularly accurate or helpful one, in my opinion, if we want to truly adopt a systems approach to the challenges that we face. Indeed a more appropriate and realistic term for what we are actually talking about might well be *product systems management* and *services systems management* because we are not, in fact, dealing with linear chains but rather with networks of people, businesses and statutory bodies interacting with each other in many complex and overlapping ways. The most important tenet of the systems approach is that a system, whether that system be a computer, a living organism, a company or an entire economy is made up of components that are interconnected and that this whole interconnected system is greater than the sum of its parts and exhibits characteristics and behaviours that emerge from this interconnectedness and do not exist, nor could even be predicted to exist at the component level. Viewing the web of connections and pathways between your suppliers, customers and other channel partners along which information, materials and money flow as a 'system' in this sense is a shift of viewpoint and perception that can be very powerful in generating creative new ideas for how to interact with the other players in the network in more innovative ways to increase speed, improve quality and gain competitiveness. In effect, these 'systems' are greater than the sum of their parts because they exhibit characteristics and qualities that emerge uniquely because of their interconnectedness and that are not present in a disconnected set of the same components.

The supply 'chain' as a system

Many complex entities such as a computer, a living organism or even a company culture are *systems* in the sense that we referred to earlier and it is fundamentally their interconnectedness that makes them so. A computer can calculate because of the way the components are assembled and connected to each other, a living organism is alive because of the way its elements and molecules are arranged and interconnected, while a company has a culture that *emerges* because of the unique arrangement and interaction of its tangible and intangible components. In summary, what makes a system a system and endows it with its unique emergent qualities are the connections between its components and the nature and quality of those connections. Likewise, supply chains, or perhaps more accurately, total product delivery systems, compete on the bases of the nature and quality of their connections. In the case of this type of business system that concern us here, the important connections are the relationships, procedures, protocols and processes that operate at the interfaces between the cooperating businesses and organizations in the system. In a practical sense for you as the owner or manager of a business, the adoption of a systems approach, to viewing your supply chain and the relationships that bind it together, provides a useful and powerful framework that will help you to deal with some of the following challenges:

- supplier development
- leveraging the capabilities of transport and logistics service providers
- developing channel partners to access distant markets
- setting up operations in overseas locations
- innovation and competition.

Let's look at just one example from each of these topics. When procuring materials from suppliers, one aspect that is often overlooked is the physical configuration of the materials from the point of view of packaging and unitization, whether that be in cases, sacks, bags or pallets. When you consider from an SCM, or systems, perspective that how the product is packed and unitized by your supplier can have efficiency and cost implication right through the chain all the way to your production process and to your distribution centre you can identify options for improvement. Supplier packaging and unitization can have a dramatic impact on transportation costs, material handling costs, warehouse utilization, facility and storage design, processing and repacking, line efficiency and so much more.

Supply chain partners

The capabilities of logistics and transport service providers are often key in the development of competitive supply chain management strategies to ensure that your products reach their destination in the quantity and quality required and in a timely manner. The relationships with these service providers tend to be stable over relatively long periods of time with constant interaction between your company and the service provider and consequently it is important that the relationship be continuously cultivated and developed. Because these logistics service providers deal with many other businesses both inside and outside your sector at home and abroad, they are systemic connectors par excellence, they can be a source of learning and innovation that you can leverage to mutual advantage through the maintenance of high-quality relationships and communications. The channel partners that help you to maintain a presence in distant markets may be agents, representatives, distributors or resellers. These are hugely important for all businesses, and especially for SMEs, that wish to enter overseas markets but who do not have the scale or volume of business, to develop and set up wholly-owned operations in the target market. Often your products and services will form part of a portfolio of options that the agent or distributor brings to market and yet from the end users' point of view, they may well be the face of your business. By taking a 'systems' view of your total product delivery system, you will be wise to consider them as such also. Consequently, the development and nurturing of the relationship with these partners, including meeting with them frequently in person, will make a tremendous difference to your success in these markets.

Setting up operations in overseas markets is a very complex and truly systemic undertaking. Multiple considerations, apart from the purely technical, come into play such as the cultural, legal, fiscal and political considerations associated with alternative location options. Once you have established overseas operations, the integration of the home and overseas elements under a coherent strategy with aligned goals and plans will also benefit tremendously from taking a systems perspective. For example, it may be that for the benefit of the whole it is necessary for some elements of the network to make some compromises and trade-offs that can be difficult to understand if viewed at the local level only, but that make sense when the overall system is considered in this *systemic* way. Innovation and competition will benefit from harnessing the knowledge, perspectives and ideas that enter the business through the interfaces at its edges, or interfaces, with all these supply chain partners, including suppliers, distribution channel partners, logistics service providers and the overseas locations themselves. This should be made purposeful and explicit to ensure that these opportunities are harnessed consistently. As the British philosopher, John Stuart Mills wrote in 1848, 'It is hardly possible to overrate the value of placing human beings in contact with persons dissimilar to themselves, with modes of thoughts and action unlike those with which they are familiar... Such communication has always been one of the primary sources of progress' (Mills, 1848).

The interface crucible: supply chain relationships where the rubber meets the road

Long-term business relationships

In today's economy, where technology and deregulation are both enabling the formation of such networks, as well as driving the need for their formation, the systems approach provided by supply chain management is a very useful and powerful tool and framework. It allows us to deal with the complexity of situation and brings to the fore the fact that it is the strength and quality of the relationships and connections that we build with other players that will ultimately determine the effectiveness and the success of our business. Some of these relationships will be long term and stable over long periods of time and others will be more transient. Take, for example, the relationship between a manufacturer in the pharmaceutical sector, a client company with whom I have consulted for many years, and a logistics services company that provides transport, warehousing and other value-added logistics services to this manufacturer. Like many of these manufacturer–logistics–services-provider relationships, this one has developed incrementally over an extended period to a degree whereby the interdependency between the parties is now quite considerable and mutually symbiotic. As manufacturing companies have increasingly preferred to focus on their core competences of product, process and R&D they have come to rely ever more on logistics services companies to handle and manage their materials requirements including the sourcing of raw materials, inbound and outbound transport, inventory management, warehousing, sampling, kitting and many other services.

Relationships and asymmetrical power balances

The difference between success and failure in these arrangements is attributable, fundamentally, to the effectiveness and quality of the relationships that have been built between the organizations. Of course, not all relationships are created equal and in business, asymmetrical power balances between supplier and customer and between different partners in strategic alliances are more the norm than the exception. We see these asymmetrical relationships all the time between manufacturers and their logistics services companies such as the one we have just referred to, as well as between suppliers and their customers, and between producers and their distribution channel partners. On both sides of the power balance, there are challenges to be overcome to ensure a successful relationship that delivers business benefits for all parties. The key questions of common objectives, shared benefits and agreed-upon metrics are crucial for the long-term sustainability of these types of business relationships. These long-term relationships can deepen and broaden over time and become strategically significant for either one, or both, the partners, as we have seen. It is imperative to take good care of these relationships and to consistently monitor that they are continuing to provide business benefits for both partners and to ensure that they do not become stale and stultified.

Short-term business relationships

While sustaining long-term strategic relationships is critical for success, an ever more common response to the rapidly changing business environment is the formation of short-term alliances designed to address specific tactical goals, projects or initiatives. In many instances, these arrangements bring together people from different disciplines who often come from different cultures and ethnic backgrounds working together across international borders. Add in long distances and different time zones and the complexities and challenges of sustaining successful working relationships increase even more. For example, in the business of engineering projects typically involve business development professionals, data analysts and computer programmers working together to develop and implement engineering design solutions. I was recently involved in a project like this where the team was composed of quite a small group of individuals working together; however, the data analysis work was carried out in Kathmandu, Nepal, the coding for the computer applications was developed in Zagreb, Croatia and the project was managed and directed from Dublin, Ireland for a client with worldwide operations. The challenges of time zone, culture, language and administrative distance all needed to be considered to ensure a successful outcome to the project. In many cases, these short-term arrangements are a one-off. Sometimes, however, the same group of people may come together several times as required for specific time-bounded projects. In all cases it is crucial to manage these relationships to leverage the strength of the diversity of the team to the benefit of all. This continuous forming and reforming of situational, inter-organizational relationships is very much akin to the way the film industry brings together multiple skills and disciplines for a definite period to produce a movie and requires very high levels of coordination, flexibility and creativity.

Fundamentals of high-quality business relationships

Whether the relationships are long term or short term there are certain fundamental characteristics or principles that characterize relationships that are strong, effective and likely to last in the case of long-term arrangements or to be re-established in the case of short-term, ad hoc arrangements. Trustworthiness and fairness are essential ingredients in good relationships. This is particularly so in the cases where the partners in the relationship hold very different proportions of power as is common in many supplier–customer relationships that we encounter in business, such as in the case of the many small suppliers of food products to the large multiple retailers. Trustworthiness has two key components: on the one hand there is trust in the sense that you expect the other person be honest and to act fairly, and on the other hand, there is the trust that they have the competence to deliver on their promises and undertakings. Absent either one of these elements, and the partner is not worthy of our trust. Fairness is also hugely important for the longevity of the relationship, particularly on the part of the partner that commands the larger proportion of the power. Whereas the smaller or weaker partner may be compelled to stick with an unfair arrangement, the sustainability of the relationship ultimately will be damaged if the arrangements are manifestly unfair.

Management of expectations

It is important also that each partner to the arrangement has realistic expectations regarding the business benefits to be obtained from the relationship. For the relationship to exist at all there must be benefits that accrue to each of the partners that are greater than the benefits that could be obtained by each partner acting alone or disintermediating the partner. It is important to negotiate and explicitly agree the expected benefits that each partner hopes to achieve so that there is transparency and mutual understanding, and so that unrealistic expectations can be avoided.

Good communication is another essential ingredient in any good relationship. In business relationships it is important to clarify what the communications protocols are and to standardize these as much as possible. This should cover what information is to be communicated, in what format and through which medium. Additionally, it should cover when and how frequently communication is to take place, as well as which people or roles are to carry out this communication. This kind of highly structured communication protocol is useful when dealing with day-to-day technical issues, where it is important to minimize ambiguity and maximize efficiency.

In addition to this highly structured communication, another element of communication that is essential and very valuable is the unstructured, spontaneous communication between people in businesses that work together that takes place in more informal setting on visits, at trade shows and exhibitions and so on. It is in these types of encounters that personal bonds are formed. When the working relationships are with people from other countries, cultures and languages it is these situations when the appreciation and understanding of diversity, the culture and language of the partners can really bear fruit in the building of empathy and rapport. The strengthening of the bonds that this achieves helps the people from the different organizations that work together to share a sense of common purpose. Inevitably there will be problems from time to time in any relationship. Mistakes are made, or outside circumstances beyond the control of the partners may simply conspire to produce undesired and unforeseen outcomes. The good work done in building trust, demonstrating fairness, developing transparency, and high-quality communication will contribute to building the empathy that is needed to get through, and get over, the difficult patches when things are not working well. For both long- and short-term business relationships, it is useful and powerful to have a pattern and structure under which these relationships can be set up, developed and managed effectively and successfully.

The seven pragmatic steps to success

Here we put forward a seven-step process with the acronym OFRIMAC – Objectives, Feasibility, Resources, Implementation, Measure, Adjust and Celebrate – to provide support and guidance in the endeavour.

1 **Objective:** What are the purpose and objectives of the relationship?

2 **Feasibility:** Are the objectives feasible and desirable?

3 **Resources:** What resources are required to set up and maintain the relationship?

4 **Implement:** How will the relationship be set up and run in practice?

5 **Measure:** What are the metrics and is the relationship delivering the expected results as defined by the objectives?

6 **Adjust:** Does the relationship need to be tweaked, developed or discontinued?

7 **Celebrate:** How do we appreciate and savour the success of the relationship?

Objective

What is the purpose of the relationship and what are the specific objectives? It is important that all relationships have a purpose and clearly defined objectives, even if, as can commonly be the case, the relationship comes about in an opportunistic or serendipitous fashion. Without clear objectives it will be impossible later to determine whether the relationship is effective and successful in delivering real business benefits because there will be no reference points against which to evaluate. For example, is the relationship expected to deliver cost advantages, improved speed to market, greater market share, higher margins, greater turnover and so on? The objectives must be defined in terms of true business outcomes such as these. In one long-standing supply chain relationship between a manufacturer and logistics service provider, I witnessed an uplift in the volume of materials required to be moved into and out of the manufacturing plant by the service provider. This gave rise to specific objectives defined in terms of throughput activity, storage space requirement, delivery time and other defined service requirements related to documentation and labelling. These are the types of specific, quantifiable objectives that contribute to the achievement of the desired business outcomes.

Feasibility

It is important to check the objectives against a set of relevant criteria to ensure that there is a good chance that the relationship will succeed in achieving its objectives and delivering the value that achieving the business outcomes is expected to deliver. For example, the objectives must be specific, they must be positive, and they must be amenable to measurement. Additionally, you need to consider how the other partner is to benefit from the relationship so that you are fully cognizant of what will contribute to its sustainability. A relationship in which a disproportionate portion of the benefit accrues to one partner only will not be sustainable. You will also need to consider how the relationship may affect other relationships and stakeholders in your supply chain and what may have to be relinquished, to achieve success. What is the upside? What is the downside? Is it worth the trouble?

By way of example, in the manufacturer–service-provider example referred to earlier, there was an important consideration in that the logistics service provider was facing two potentially undesirable knock-on effects from the proposed changes. One was that the increased space requirement had the potential to negatively impact other, unconnected, revenue-generating contracts that they were undertaking for different customers and the second was the possibility of having to introduce a night shift for which they had no precedent among their workforce.

Resources

What resources in terms of time, people, skills and technology will be required to achieve the objectives? Do you have them? Can you access or develop them? How long will it take to marshal the resources you require to implement the relationship effectively? One of the key resources required in our example was better quality information on the manufacturer's requirements in terms of timeliness and visibility to the service provider. To obtain this, it required the deepening of the integration between the two companies in the form of an agreed communications protocol together with retraining of key individuals in both companies who would work together on a daily basis to ensure effective information provision and transfer.

Implementation

What are the most effective ways of setting up and maintaining the relationship? Who specifically will be involved? How will people interact? What will they be required to do on a day-to-day basis? What will be the processes and procedures that will guide and facilitate the tasks that need to be performed? In our example, a detailed plan of implementation through ramp-up, go-live and bedding in was developed and implemented by a team composed of members from both organizations working in close collaboration right through the set-up and into steady-state operations.

Measure

How will we know that we are making progress towards the objectives and that we are operating to the standard required? It is crucially important to be continually informed through both objective and subjective measures and feedback at multiple levels regarding how well the relationship is achieving the objectives and delivering the expected business benefits for the parties involved. In our example, measures were established at multiple levels, ranging from daily work-plan schedules visible on the warehouse floor, to standard daily templates and reports visible to key stakeholders as well as frequent review and feedback sessions between the key managers of both companies.

Adapt

Relationships are in continuous evolution in response to the changing needs of the participants and changes in the systemic environment. To be effective, whether the relationships are short term or long term, they must have the flexibility to adapt and adjust to changing circumstances. In our example, several precedents were set for communication and information sharing between the two companies. These were later extended and transferred into other initiatives between the two companies and that allowed the relationship and interdependency of the companies to increase while maintaining high levels of trust and confidence in the business benefits delivered for both sides.

Celebrate

Relationships are about people, and people like to know when their efforts are making a positive contribution. It is important to mark these achievements by celebrating in tangible ways that are meaningful to the people involved. In the example, several tangible rewards, recognitions and events hosted in the facilities of both partner companies take place on an ongoing basis to ensure that successfully achieved milestones, standards and outcomes were explicitly recognized and celebrated.

Summary

In this opening chapter we have set the scene for international business and the relationships on which it is built in the context of the process of globalization of the world economy, driven by innovations in information and communications technology (ICT), the deregulation of international trade and finance and developments in transportation technology and infrastructures. We have seen that notwithstanding the fact that trade globalization in particular has been experiencing some headwinds since 2016 due to protectionism and the increase in some trade tariffs between the major global trading blocs of North America, Europe and East Asia and the fact that globalization was always an incomplete and unevenly distributed process across the world, that international trade and international business relationship will continue to be an increasingly important factor for companies of all sizes in the future. Indeed, competition from foreign firms in the home markets of many SMEs is compelling them to internationalize their own businesses on both the supply and distribution sides to remain competitive and thrive in the future.

We have also discussed who the concept of the supply chain and the suite of tools, techniques and technologies referred to as supply chain management provides a very powerful framework and reference to enable companies to approach the challenges of the internationalization of their business networks in practical and pragmatic ways. One of the salient characteristics of supply chain management that we have highlighted is the fact that it brings a systems approach to the consideration of the behaviour of supply chains and how to act on them to achieve desired business outcomes. By systemic we mean that these systems need to be viewed in the content of the whole network of players involved and how the connections, interactions and relationships between them are designed, set up and managed, whether they be in long-term stable working relationships or in short-term project-type arrangements. We rounded out the chapter by setting out a practical and pragmatic approach to formulating and implementing effective international business relationships based around the seven steps encapsulated in the acronym OFRIMAC, that is, Objectives, Feasibility, Resources, Implement, Measure, Adjust and Celebrate. Following a structured approach in this manner will help ensure that important steps and considerations are not omitted and that many of the common pitfalls are avoided. In the subsequent chapters of the book, we will return in more depth and detail to many of the themes raised in this opening chapter.

References

Deutsche Welle (2017) Angela Merkel welcomes US offer to resume TTIP talks. Available from www.dw.com/en/angela-merkel-welcomes-us-offer-to-resume-ttip-talks/a-39446579 [last accessed 1 June 2018]

DublinAirport.com (2015) Ryanair Celebrates 30th anniversary. Available from www.dublinairport.com/latest-news/detail/2015/07/08/ryanair-celebrates-30th-anniversary [last accessed 20 May 2018]

FAO (2015) Food and Agriculture Organization Fisheries and Aquaculture Consumption of Fish and Seafood. Available from www.fao.org/fishery/statistics/global-consumption/en [last accessed 10 January 2016]

Ghemawat, P (2018) *The New Global Road Map: Enduring strategies for turbulent times*, Harvard Business Review Press, Boston, MA

IMF (2018) International Monetary Fund: World Economic Outlook Database, International Monetary Fund, 7 June 2018. Available from www.imf.org [last accessed 27 May 2018]

Mills, JS (1848) *Principles of Political Economy with Some of their Applications to Social Philosophy*, Elibron Classics, London

World Trade Organization (2017) Trade Statistical Review 2017. Available from www.wto.org/english/res_e/statis_e/wts2017_e/wts2017_e.pdf [last accessed 20 June 2018]

The world is not flat

02

Geography still matters

Where in the world?

While globalization is a manifest reality, it is not spread evenly around the world. Some places are much more connected and integrated into the global economy than others. Some aspects of business, such as finance, are far more globalized than others, such as labour. While great benefits in cost, innovation and speed can be obtained through the development of global supply chains there are also considerable risks that need to be taken into account associated with the quality and availability of infrastructure, access to skills, exchange rates fluctuations, natural disasters, terrorism, and many other factors that can add uncertainty and complexity to the mix. You need to do your homework to understand the world that you are venturing out into. In 2005, the *New York Times'* journalist and author, Thomas L. Friedman published a fascinating book called *The World is Flat: A brief history of the twenty-first century* (Friedman, 2005). In his book, Friedman explains how competition and global business opportunities are becoming more equal across the world or, as he puts it, 'the global economic playing field is being levelled'. This is only partly true, and the effects of globalization are unevenly spread across the globe.

The economic, legal and fiscal frameworks, and the consequent ease or difficulty of doing business and integrating material and information flows into global supply chains and networks still vary greatly from place to place. The degree to which a given place in the world is integrated into the globalized economic framework is a complex function of the human and economic geography of that place – yes, even in the interconnected world of the 21st century, geography does still matter; in fact, it matters very much. This consideration is extremely important for you as business owners and managers, because the choices you make as your businesses internationalize to take advantage of the opportunities presented by a globalized economy regarding where and with whom you form working partnerships, locate overseas resellers and distributors, distribution centres, production plants, corporate headquarters and research and development facilities will have a major impact on the sustainability and continuity of your business in the face of an ever-changing global environment.

Why do corporations internationalize?

Many larger companies in the developed economies of North America, Western Europe and Japan, such as General Electric, Royal Dutch Shell, BP, Toyota and Walmart, since the middle of the 20th century have transformed themselves into truly multinational corporations (MNCs). These are organizations, headquartered in one country but with, whole or partially owned subsidiaries located in other countries and with complex global arrangements based on a mix of joint ventures, strategic alliances, mergers and acquisitions that have been one of the key factors in the transformation of the global economy over the last 50 years and the setting of new rules of the global game. The motivations for the internationalization of these large corporations includes the search for new growth opportunities with the saturation of home markets, the desire to escape the constraints of the high costs of organized labour at home particularly for manufacturing processes where the application of new technologies is difficult, the need to overcome protectionist policies in important overseas markets and, perhaps most controversially of all, the ability to plan tax affairs in ways more favourable to the global organization by leveraging tax arbitrage opportunities between different jurisdictions. The advances in communications and transport technologies combined with international financial deregulation and the removal of barriers to international trade and investment have both enabled and accelerated the process.

In some regards there has been a mutually beneficial symbiotic relationship between developed and developing economies whereby corporations in highly developed economies in North America and Europe have been able to concentrate high value-added manufacturing operations in these home regions creating high-paid jobs where new processes and techniques are industrialized and perfected. The manufacture of products that have reached maturity in the product lifecycle and whose manufacturing processes have been perfected are then relocated to overseas locations providing industrial development and job opportunities in those locations. This enables competitively priced products to be brought to consumers in developed markets while allowing increased focus on innovation and creativity at the home base. To illustrate this point, it is noteworthy that, while China and the US have similar figures for absolute manufacturing value added, the US manages to do this with seven times fewer people employed in manufacturing (IMF, 2018).

While this process provides clear advantages for corporations, consumers and the developing economies, it has led to a significant reduction in the numbers of people employed in manufacturing in the developed economies. In the US, the number of peoples employed in manufacturing dropped by over 30 per cent between 2000 and 2010, though it has recovered somewhat to a position in 2018 where it is just 25 per cent off the 2000 figure (Bureau of Labor Statistics, 2018), while manufacturing output has continued to rise. This is due to a complex combination of technological advances and the moving of production offshore and from traditional locations within developed countries to new locations within the same country. For example, the shift in the US from the Michigan–Ohio–Pennsylvania arc to new locations in states in the south and southwest such as Georgia, Texas and Arizona (Schneider, 2017). As this transformation has progressed, driven and led in the first instance by the developed economy MNCs, it has compelled suppliers and competitors to follow suit as they strive to compete with or to support the MNCs. Over time, organizations originating in developing economies such as India, China, Brazil and Mexico have in turn internationalized and become MNCs in their own right and now compete actively in the home markets of the original MNCs particularly in North America and Europe. Companies such as Bimbo from Mexico, Tata from India and Haier from China are among these emerging market multinationals that are disrupting competition in the developed markets of America and Europe and becoming household names. At this point in time, these multinational corporations with origins in both the developed and developing economies account for 70 to 80 per cent of world trade (UNCTAD, 2017).

Threat and opportunity

These transformations, which have gathered pace over the last 20 years, constitute both a threat and an opportunity for all businesses, whether they compete in international markets and, whether, up to now they have been happy and successful to operate and grow profitably within local, regional or national markets. Notwithstanding the fact that some of the manifestations of globalization such as international trade volumes have been sluggish or declining since the Great Recession of 2008 (WTO, 2017), and free trade has been falling out of political favour in many of the developed economies, the stay-at-home insular approach is becoming ever more difficult to sustain. This is because, the genie is already out of the bottle with regard to the opportunities for growth and profitability that companies can access by internationalizing and also because consumers have become accustomed to an unending supply of innovative, quality products at competitive prices made possible by the globalization of business. Add to this the fact that globalization is a very uneven process across the world, and one that has not been as deeply or as broadly developed as many perceive. This means that there is still enormous value to be tapped by companies that learn effectively how to leverage the advantages of internationalization through the selection of the best locations to do business and through building supply chain solutions to underpin these international business strategies.

Businesses adjust to geopolitical 'weather'

My prediction is that businesses will find ways to access international markets, whether by trade, investment or partnerships, despite the political and regulatory barriers that may be thrown up in the coming years. They will continue to seek new markets for growth and profitability and the consumers in these markets will continue to demand that their needs and wants be met. Globalization will not so much recede as it will morph into a new form to fit around the new regulatory and political environment that is emerging. In recent years, since the global recession of 2008, while international trade in goods recovered only slowly and currently is stagnant, the international flows of capital, people and most importantly information have continued to increase (Ghemawat, 2018).

Of course, global economic integration has happened before. In the early 20th century the global economy had reached a point of considerable integration with the major centres of Europe, Asia and the Americas tied together by regular freight transport routes based on steamships, greatly facilitated by the opening of the Suez Canal in 1869 and the Panama Canal in 1914. Telegraph networks provided the communications backbone to this globalized economy of the early 20th century. The further integration of the world economy was unexpectedly interrupted by a succession of cataclysmic events over a 30-year period starting with the First World War, 1914 to 1918, followed by the Great Depression in the late 1920s and 1930s and the Second World War from 1939 to 1945. Indeed, the value of global trade reached by 1913, was not attained again until the early 1970s. Since then, and until 2008 global trade grew almost six-fold (Ortiz-Ospina and Roser, 2018) outpacing economic growth by a factor of two to one during the 1990s and experiencing a dramatic spurt in the early 2000s before stalling with the onset of the Great Recession in 2008 followed by decreases in several successive years and only a very anaemic recovery after 2012. Indeed, through 2014, 2015 and 2016 growth in global trade slowed to almost zero (WTO, 2017).

It is true that in the current political and economic context, there is growing opposition to global free trade agreements with both the

Trans-Pacific Partnership (TPP) between the US and a number of Pacific Rim countries and the Transatlantic Trade and Investment Partnership (TTIP) between the US and the European Union running into strong opposition which has so far delayed their adoption and implementation. Even the Comprehensive Economic and Trade Agreement (CETA) between Canada and European Union that was negotiated over a period of seven years was only signed in October 2016 after last-minute opposition from the regional parliament in Belgium's Wallonia had delayed the originally planned sign-off date (Zalan, 2016). The reality for businesses on the ground, however, is that with free trade agreements or without them, consumers around the world will continue to seek high-quality products at competitive prices and businesses from all over the world will seek to gain access to international markets, whether by trade, investment or acquisition to grow and thrive. This is the challenge that we, as business managers and owners need to contend with. Therefore, the need to look beyond the home environment to head off the threat posed by outside competition and take advantage of the opportunities of globalization to access new options for supply and for growth is becoming ever more urgent for an increasing number of businesses, whether they like it or not.

Globalization in the longer term

Taking a long-term view of the process of globalization, if we consider that even a social, economic and political cataclysm of the magnitude of that which befell the world in the first half of the 20th century was unable to derail the process of globalization for very long, the chances are that this is a meta-process that is unfolding above and beyond the short-term political and economic crises being experienced at the current time (Dass, 2011). As business people, this is something that we are going to need to learn to recognize and to cope with, so that we can effectively mitigate the threats that it poses and take advantage of the opportunities that it offers. Indeed, to adapt Leon Trotsky's, perhaps misattributed, sinister reference to war, you may not be interested in globalization, but globalization is interested in you. To be successful in this endeavour, it is inevitable that new and unfamiliar relationships and alliances that extend across international borders will need to be formed and nurtured with a wide range of partners including suppliers, service providers and state agencies. Judicious selection of where and with whom these relationships are established will be a fundamental competitive differentiator between businesses large and small as the risks and complexities of international business relationships will continue to pose real challenges for companies. Consequently, it is becoming imperative that companies of all sizes acquire the skills and wherewithal to formulate and implement strategies that incorporate value-added knowledge and intelligence about the threats and opportunities associated with place, to enable them to engage successfully with the not-so-flat world of globalization, where geography does still matter. This capability will be essential whether they wish to source supplies abroad more competitively, export to new high-growth international markets, negotiate distribution contracts with global logistics service providers or establish their own manufacturing and distribution operations overseas through the establishment of subsidiaries, joint ventures or strategic partnerships. Complacency will not be an option and ignorance will be no excuse.

Nodes, hubs and poles of attraction

As the world economy has globalized and integrated, two countervailing processes have been ongoing simultaneously – the processes of concentration and dispersion. On the one hand, there has been a marked dispersion of economic activities such as manufacturing across the globe to the newly industrialized economies in Asia and Latin America and away from traditional centres in Europe, North America and Japan (Ghemawat, 2018). Firstly, in the 1970s this was driven by large corporations from the developed economies, investing in productive capacity inside the territories of countries such as Brazil, with large internal markets with highly protective trade barriers. They did this to overcome the wall of protective trade barriers to gain access to these large and developing consumer markets and to fuel their continued corporate growth which had largely stalled at home due to market saturation. Thereafter, as financial deregulation, the lifting of trade barriers and technological innovation in transport and communications, progressed apace through the 1980s and 1990s, many multinational corporations realized that they could implement a new geographical division of labour by adopting operational strategies whereby they offshored labour-intensive, low value-add, aspects of their production to low-wage countries, moving raw materials, semi-finished and finished products across the globe from their places of production to their places of consumption, giving rise to complex supply chains or product system networks coordinated and managed from global hubs in the developed world.

Dispersion of manufacturing activities

This enabled these corporations to extract certain elements of their production from relatively high-wage locations, with organized labour in the developed world and relocate them to low-cost locations elsewhere. A relatively small group of countries, including Brazil, Mexico, China, India, Thailand, South Korea, Indonesia, Malaysia, Taiwan, Hong Kong, and Singapore were the main beneficiaries of this dispersion of production accounting for some 75 per cent of manufactured exports (Ghemawat, 2018). The reasons for their success were multiple and varied on an individual basis and included factors of scale, location, infrastructural heritage, labour supply, and the role of the state. Therefore, while a global dispersion of production did occur, this dispersion was concentrated within a relatively small number of global locations. Vast areas of the globe have remained relatively untouched by the benefits of globalization, most notably Sub-Saharan Africa. Furthermore, those locations in both the developed and developing economies that were already the nodes and hubs of the global networks have tended to act as magnets for further localized development of logistical infrastructure, global and regional corporate headquarters and centres of distribution, research and development, and finance. In effect, those places that started with an initial advantage have tended to deepen that advantage over time.

Concentration of global economic hubs

Places like New York, London and Toyko have become pre-eminent world cities and global economic centres. Other locations such as Singapore, Dubai, Hong Kong, Shanghai, Paris and Chicago have also consolidated their positions as major centres of the global economy. The logistical and transport networks of the world have also gravitated to certain nodes and hubs where infrastructure, skills and service capability in specialized areas have reached critical mass. These include places such as Singapore, Rotterdam, Memphis, Panama, Shenzhen, Los Angeles, and others that concentrate the greater part of the world's logistical capability and expertise (Ghemawat and Altman, 2016). When considering the internationalization of your business, whether through exports, or direct investment in manufacturing and distribution capabilities, these are extremely pertinent factors to consider. On the one hand, it is important to note those locations that are already global centres in which the capabilities and infrastructure make it easier and more economical to internationalize successfully. On the other hand, it is important to understand that there are up and coming locations, not widely known and appreciated, that may offer significant future advantages to companies that have taken the time and the trouble to carry out the pertinent research, analyse the evolving trends and identify the opportunities that apply to their particular business and circumstances.

The key point is, however, that regions of economic power worldwide are spread very unevenly, they are usually centred on a strong urban nucleus and located in North America, Europe and East Asia. The likelihood is that the dominance of these global economic powerhouses will increase in the years to come due to the initial advantage conferred by the critical mass of income, infrastructure, innovation and economic activity that they have accumulated. The University of Toronto's Martin Prosperity Institute (MPI) Research Team has produced a ranking of the world's most powerful economic cities (Florida, 2015). The ranking is based on a diverse range of measures covering aspects of each city such as competitiveness, financial power, equity and quality of life, as well as overall economic clout. Perhaps unsurprisingly, the top five cities in the ranking

Table 2.1   The world's most powerful economic cities

City	2015 Rank	Total Score	2012 Rank
New York	1	48	1
London	2	40	2
Tokyo	3	29	3
Hong Kong	4	21	4
Paris	5	19	4
Singapore	6	17	7
Los Angeles	7	13	9
Seoul	8	11	11
Vienna	9	10	–
Stockholm	10	9	–
Toronto	10	9	18
Chicago	12	8	6
Zurich	13	6	10
Sydney	14	5	–
Helsinki	14	5	–
Dublin	16	4	–
Osaka-Kobe	16	4	15
Boston	18	3	11
Oslo	18	3	–
Beijing	18	3	11
Shanghai	18	3	8
Geneva	22	2	–
Washington	23	1	14
San Francisco	23	1	–
Moscow	23	1	–

are New York, London, Tokyo, Hong Kong and Paris. The top 25 cities in the ranking include 10 European cities, seven North American cities, seven Asian cities and one city in Australia. Table 2.1 shows the complete MPI top 25 ranking.

These places are the locations at which much of the world's innovation, R&D, financial and corporate headquarters activity takes place. These are the centres of global business. While many of these centres are very well known and long-standing global business centres, it is interesting to see the emergence of some relative new-comers including the likes of Stockholm, Sydney, Dublin and Moscow among others.

World Bank Logistics Performance Index

Another interesting perspective on the global centres of business operations is provided by the World Bank's Logistics Performance Index (World Bank, 2016). From the point of view of those considerations that are of relevance to the siting of global operations for manufacturing or distribution, this is a comprehensive index that provides essential insights on the performance of all countries.

This index includes the following considerations:

- efficiency of the customs clearance process
- quality of roads, railroads, ports and information technology
- ease of arranging competitively priced international shipments
- ability to track and trace consignments
- competence and quality of logistics services such as transport, warehousing and customs brokerage
- timeliness of shipments reaching destination within scheduled delivery time.

In the World Bank's 2016 Logistics Performance Index (World Bank, 2016), the countries with the five highest LPI scores were Germany, Luxembourg, Sweden, the Netherlands and Singapore. These are countries with highly competitive and integrated economies that demonstrate a consistent level of excellence regarding logistics and supply chain services, infrastructure and know-how essential for successful business operations. Table 2.2 shows the top 25 ranked countries on the LPI index.

Another important aspect to consider when evaluating global locations is the openness of the economy to international trade. The International Chamber of Commerce (ICC) produces an Open Markets Index of those countries most open to trade (International Chamber of Commerce, 2015). The top ranked economies in the

Table 2.2   The Logistics Performance Index
country ranking

Country	LPI Rank	LPI score
Germany	1	4.23
Luxembourg	2	4.22
Sweden	3	4.20
Netherlands	4	4.19
Singapore	5	4.14
Belgium	6	4.11
Austria	7	4.10
United Kingdom	8	4.07
Hong Kong	9	4.07
United States	10	3.99
Switzerland	11	3.99
Japan	12	3.97
UAE	13	3.94
Canada	14	3.93
Finland	15	3.92
France	16	3.90
Denmark	17	3.82
Ireland	18	3.79
Australia	19	3.79
South Africa	20	3.78
Italy	21	3.76
Norway	22	3.73
Spain	23	3.73
South Korea	24	3.72
Taiwan	25	3.70

ICC's 2015 Open Markets Index are Singapore and Hong Kong and
these are the only economies categorized as 'Most Open' with scores
of 5.5 out of 6.0. The next category of countries is classified as demonstrating 'Above Average Openness' with scores of between 4.0 and
5.0 out of 6.0. This group is headed by a group of small European
economies, which includes Luxembourg (4.9), Belgium (4.8), the
Netherlands (4.8), Ireland (4.7) and Switzerland (4.7). The rest of
this group is comprised mostly of northern and western European

countries including Germany and the United Kingdom, as well as the developed economies of New Zealand, Australia, Canada, and the developing economies of UAE, Taiwan, Chile and Malaysia.

DHL Global Connectedness Index

Yet another perspective on the connectedness to the global economy of various locations around the world is provided by the DHL Global Connectedness Index produced by Pankaj Ghemawat and Steven A Altman (2016). DHL is global logistics company and part of the Deutsche Post DHL Group. The advances in logistics capabilities and the development of global logistics service providers such as DHL and others has been one of the key enablers of worldwide supply chains of the MNCs that have underpinned the development of economic globalization in recent decades. In the 2016 edition of the DHL Global Connectedness Index countries and cities are scored on both the breadth and the depth of their globalization. In the index, the depth of globalization of a location refers to the relative intensity of its international interactions with respect to its domestic interactions, and the breath of globalization refers to physical and cultural distance over which these interactions take place. On the basis of the DHL Index, the top three most connected countries in the world are the Netherlands, Singapore and Ireland. These are followed by Switzerland, Luxembourg, Belgium, Germany, the United Kingdom, Denmark and the United Arab Emirates. In terms of cities, the index identifies several global hotspots; these are the cities with 'the most intense flows of trade, capital, people and information compared to their internal activity'. The top three global hotspots in 2016 were Singapore, Manama and Hong Kong, followed by Dubai, Amsterdam, Tallinn, Dublin, Geneva, Abu Dhabi and Skopje.

Doing your homework – seven steps to success

So where do you start, when looking to formulate and implement an international operating strategy for your business that is going to enable you to compete and thrive in the future? Notwithstanding the fact that we are now seeing the emergence of so-called 'born global' start-ups, the plain fact is that many firms' international journeys begin opportunistically or serendipitously rather than being the fruit of a structured desktop exercise in formal strategy formulation. For firms that have developed in the traditional way, doing business in their home markets, a meeting at a trade fair, seminar or exhibition or a referral from a supplier or a customer may lead the company into its first opportunities with overseas suppliers or customers. In the first instance, the company uses the existing internal skills and capabilities to deal with this new opportunity in a learn-as-you-go mode. If the opportunity is promising and develops further, the learning becomes codified and specific functions and departments for international procurement or international sales and exports may be formalized and the importance of the international aspect of the business grows over time, and knowledge, skills and capabilities are built and internalized. In some cases, businesses will continue with purchasing and selling from home-country in the form of straightforward imports and exports whereas in others, they may identify further value-adding opportunities to invest directly in some overseas markets with wholly-owned production and distribution facilities, joint ventures or acquisitions.

Adopting a structured approach to internationalization

However, given the pace of change in all spheres of human activity from the technological advances that are bringing us Manufacturing 4.0 to the geopolitical shifts being experienced in Europe, Asia and the Americas, wherever you are in the internationalization journey, whether you are already exporting or operating part or wholly-owned subsidiaries in overseas markets or indeed if you have not even started the process of internationalizing your business, it can be very beneficial to take a structured and comprehensive approach to formulating and implementing the future development of your international operating strategy. A useful seven-step framework to use is one that takes you through a clarification of business objectives and what the achievement of those objectives will mean for the business, an assessment of current position with respect to the gap that separates you from the achievement of those objectives, options generating of initiatives that can achieve those objectives.

1 Objectives – clarification of objectives and business value.

2 Present – assessment of the current state and gap with respect to the objectives.

3 Analysis – development and analysis of options to achieve the objectives.

4 Evaluation – development of measures and criteria for evaluating options.

5 Selection – choosing and prioritizing initiatives for implementation.

6 Implementation – planning and executing selected initiatives with allocated resources.

7 Review and repeat – assess and evaluate results and repeat process in cycle of continuous advancement.

Objectives as business-relevant outcomes

When considering your internationalization strategy, it is important to take a structured and comprehensive approach to consider the business objectives that you seek to achieve and to articulate the tangible and intangible business benefits that you will obtain by reaching these objectives. In the process of formulating business objectives, it is important to frame these in terms of business outcomes that will deliver real business value to the firm; that is, things that are desirable 'ends' in and of themselves such as market access, profitability, efficiency, growth and so on and not in terms of 'means' such as technology, systems, equipment and so on. These things are not business outcomes and represent no value in and of themselves. They are just a means to an end – if you are not explicitly clear about what that end is you may end up focusing resource and effort on the wrong means. This process of clarification of objectives and expected benefits will help to give form to the international operational strategy that is best going to enable you to reach your business goals. However, it is true as I mentioned earlier that in many instances, the internationalization of a business comes about, not through a structured strategy formulation and implementation but rather in response to some random opportunity or serendipity such as meeting a new prospect at a trade exhibition or a referral from a satisfied customer in your home market. Nonetheless, and no matter where you are at on this journey, or indeed if you have not even started, it will be highly beneficial to pause, take stock and spend time clarifying objectives and what the achievement of these objectives will mean for the business.

Holistic analysis and options

Once objectives have been clearly determined, the next step is to holistically assess the current state of the business with respect to the gap that exists between the current position and the desired future position regarding the overseas markets of interest. Some of the considerations to examine include the following:

- regulatory requirements – customs, tax, security
- logistical considerations and connectedness of the overseas market to the global economy, transport modes and routes to market
- availability of external facilitators – logistics service providers and their capabilities, financial services, cloud-based information technology services, social/professional networks and media
- international free trade agreements between your home country and target market
- language and business culture – need for local representatives or managers
- ownership and governance – need for local partners and legal representation
- repatriation of profits and currency considerations
- support available from embassies, development agencies, industry associations and chambers of commerce.

Once current state capabilities have been comprehensively assessed, it is then time to develop the options for the various ways and means that the objectives can be delivered for the business. Typical options that arise include:

- moving from direct export to customers to appointing in-market agents, distributors, or resellers;
- leveraging external facilitators such as logistics service providers to manage material flows and distribution;
- seeking of joint venture or acquisition opportunities;
- setting up of wholly owned manufacturing and distribution facilities; and
- developing a geographic strategy for product lifecycle management, eg R&D and process development at home with mature product production switching to overseas locations.

Evaluation and selection based on relevant criteria

For the evaluation stage, it is crucially important to develop relevant criteria and metrics that are holistic and appropriately weighted and that can be used to consider the advantages and disadvantages of pursuing different courses of action to achieve the objectives. Thereafter, as a function of the speed and leverage provided by the various options, the most advantageous can be selected for prioritized implementation with the resources available. Ideally, this is an unending process, that continues through many iterations as the business develops and adjusts to the ever-changing external environment. For example, in some manufacturing sectors overseas, such as parts and components production, overseas manufacturing strategies implemented as recently as two or three years ago are now being re-assessed in the light of recent significant developments in 3D printing, which will soon enable a wide range of items to be manufactured quickly and efficiently in a range of materials that up to very recent times was not possible. Wage increases in the coastal regions of China are also fuelling changes in strategies with producers moving operations to regions of China further west and to other countries in South East Asia.

Summary

In this chapter, we have seen how globalization is a complex phenomenon that has morphed and changed over the last one hundred years. It is a process that is very real and influential in the world economy and yet whose extent is sometimes exaggerated and overestimated by critics and supporters alike. We have argued that one of the manifestations of globalization, the internationalization of business operations, provides significant opportunities for businesses of all sizes to develop value-adding strategies by leveraging the availability and power of a wide range of external facilitators to take advantage of many unexploited opportunities in business internationalization. Several key points stand out:

- The globalization of the world economy is very uneven (the world is not flat). Parts of Europe, East Asia and North America centred on major urban nuclei are the most globalized parts of the world.

- The current wave of globalization since the end of the Second World War has been driven primarily by three fundamental factors:

    i   advances in information and communications technology;

    ii deregulation of trade and financial services; and

    iii innovations in transport technology and infrastructure.

- The process of economic globalization and the internationalization of business operations was led primarily by multinational corporations from the developed economies of North America, Western Europe and Japan. These have been joined by newer MNCs from developing economies such as Russia, China and Mexico in recent times and now due to technological advances and the growing capabilities of external facilitators the advantages of the internationalization of business operations is opening up to an ever-wider range of firms including small- and medium-sized enterprises.

- Globalization constitutes both a threat and an opportunity for companies and for national economies. Some regions have seen rising unemployment and industrial decline while consumers have benefited from more competitively priced products while other regions of the world have benefited from industrial development and rising affluence.

- Any business, no matter what stage of the internationalization process it finds itself can benefit from applying a structured approach to formulating and implementing its future international operations strategy.

- Rapidly changing external conditions, technological, financial and geopolitical mean that international business strategies require constant reassessment and evaluation to ensure relevance and sustainability,

- Businesses need to develop new skills, and capabilities and acquire new knowledge and competences to enable them effectively develop and implement international operating strategies to ensure that they will thrive into the future.

References

Bureau of Labor Statistics (2018) Employment, Hours, and Earnings from the Current Employment Statistics surveys (National), available from https://data.bls.gov/pdq/SurveyOutputServlet [last accessed 10 August 2018]

Dass, DK (2011) Conceptual Globalism and Globalization: An Initiation, p 27. University of Warwick, United Kingdom

Florida, R (2015) Sorry, London: New York is the World's Most Powerful City. Available from www.citylab.com/life/2015/03/sorry-london-new-york-is-the-worlds-most-economically-powerful-city/386315/ [last accessed 12 January 2016]

Friedman, Thomas L (2005) *The World is Flat: A brief history of the twenty-first century*, Ferrar, Straus and Giroux, New York

Ghemawat, P (2018) *The New Global Road Map: Enduring Strategies for Turbulent Times*, Harvard Business Review Press, Boston, MA

Ghemawat, P and Altman, SA (2016) *DHL Global Connectedness Index: The State of Globalization in an Age of Ambiguity*, Deutsche Post DHL Group, Bonn, Germany

IMF (2018) *World Economic Outlook, April 2018: Cyclical Upswing, Structural Change*, available from www.imf.org/en/Publications/WEO/Issues/2018/03/20/world-economic-outlook-april-2018 [last accessed 7 July 2018]

International Chamber of Commerce (2015) ICC Open Markets Index, 3rd Edition. Available from https://iccwbo.org/publication/icc-open-markets-index-3rd-edition-2015/. [last accessed 2 February 2016]

Ortiz-Ospina, E and Roser, M (2018) 'International Trade'. Published online at OurWorldInData.org. Available from https://ourworldindata.org/international-trade [last accessed 11 August 2018]

Schneider, H (2017) U.S. South, not just Mexico stands in the way of Rust Belt jobs revival, 04/17. Available from www.reuters.com/article/us-usa-trump-south-insight/u-s-south-not-just-mexico-stands-in-way-of-rust-belt-jobs-revival-idUSKBN1790HO [last accessed 12 August 2018]

UNCTAD (2017) 80% of trade takes place in 'value chains' linked to transnational corporations. Available from http://unctad.org/en/pages/PressRelease.aspx?OriginalVersionID=113 [last accessed 2 June 2018]

WTO (2017) World Trade Statistical Review 2017. Available from www.wto.org/english/res_e/statis_e/wts2017_e/wts17_toc_e.htm [last accessed 8 August 2018]

World Bank (2016) Logistics Performance Index. Available from https://lpi.worldbank.org/international/global [last accessed 12 June 2017]

Zalan, E (2016) Wallonia hinders Canada-EU trade deal, 14/10. Available from https://euobserver.com/political/135507 [last accessed 12 December 2017]

Culture 03
An evolutionary strategy for success

What is culture?

The human innovation that we call 'culture' is what has enabled Homo sapiens as a species to spread across the globe and adapt successfully in many different environments, climates and terrains (Pagel, 2012). It has been a highly successful strategy that illustrates the innate flexibility and creativity of human beings. However, as a species, while we have an astonishing capacity to take on a bewildering diversity of cultures, as individuals we are highly invested with the particular culture or cultures that we happen to belong to. In a world of globalized working in which we depend for our success on the quality of our relationships with people in multiple organizations in many different countries, our innate attachment to our own culture may become an inadvertent barrier to our own success. I don't argue that we need to abandon our own cultural identity to sustain successful supply chain relationships but we do need to learn how to build trust and rapport effectively with people who belong to cultures other than our own. If we do, I believe that we will be dramatically more successful in our international business dealings as well as gaining a far richer and more complex satisfaction from the work that we do with our international supply chain partners.

But what exactly is culture and how can it be defined? I often like to think of culture in the simplest sense as just 'the way we do things around here'. Another great and succinct definition of culture that goes a bit deeper, provided by Alan Weiss, the world-renowned business consultant and president of Summit Consulting, is that culture is the set of beliefs that governs behaviour (Weiss and Khan, 2009). This link between belief and behaviour is crucial, given that people's belief systems are generally very stable. This helps to explain to some degree why cultures can be so durable over time and difficult to change. From a business point of view this is significant because it helps us to see that if we want to understand why people act the way they do, then we need to know something about the underlying beliefs that are shaping their actions. In business, this is challenging enough when dealing with supply chain partners such as suppliers, customers and service providers within our own countries, who share the same background national culture that we do, however, when we are engaged in transactions, collaborations and partnerships with supply chain partners across international borders this can become a fraught and daunting prospect indeed.

The largest fast-food service company in Asia, the Philippines-based Jollibee Foods Corporation headed by Tony Tan Caktiong, began to expand out of its home base of the Philippines with its trademark hamburger restaurants in the 1980s through a series of joint ventures arrangements with overseas business partners (Bartlett and Beamish, 2014). Its first foreign ventures were established in other southeast Asian countries such as Singapore, Indonesia and Brunei, as well as further north in Hong Kong and Taiwan. What the company found as it embarked on these new initiatives was that its tried and tested formula of expansion that had worked so well inside the Philippines, having reached a total of some 60 outlets by the late 80s, of which nearly 50 were franchises operated by local business partners, was that they needed to adapt their modus operandi significantly in order to be successful with their foreign operations. In each new location, the company had to deal with business partners from very different backgrounds and national cultures from the Philippines, operating in jurisdictions with different legal and regulatory frameworks that impacted everything from business strategy and operating control to store design and build, as well as staff recruitment, training and retention. Notwithstanding early mistakes and setbacks, the company persevered and adapted, eventually setting up a dedicated International Division staffed with people with specific skill sets honed to deal with the unique challenges posed by the development and implementation of overseas franchises and joint ventures. Today, Jollibee operates 3,000 outlets worldwide in markets across Southeast

Asia, Mainland China, the Middle East and North America with total revenues of some $2 billion.

'There is more than water between them and us'

The Jonathan Lewis-directed movie, *The Treaty*, made in 1991, tells the story of the negotiations in 1921 between the delegation of the incipient Irish Republic and the British government of Lloyd George, and is a gripping piece of historical drama depicting the negotiations that led to the Anglo-Irish Agreement that brought the Irish War of Independence that erupted in 1919 to a close after almost three years of conflict. In one scene, following a particularly testy exchange between the two negotiating teams, Michael Collins, one of the chief negotiators on the Irish side played by actor Brendan Gleeson, turns to one of his negotiating-team colleagues and says to him *'you know what it is? there's far more than water between them and us'*. What Collins was trying to highlight to his colleague, was the metaphorical ocean, and not just the literal Irish Sea that existed between the different world views, beliefs, values and ways of working of the two sets of negotiators, which was going to make this negotiation very tricky and potentially very dangerous. On the one hand, a group of idealistic Irish nationalists, Celtic revivalists and academics and on the other the embodiment of the British Empire at its zenith represented by Prime Minister, David Lloyd George, his Secretary of State for the Colonies, Winston Churchill, the Lord Chancellor, Lord Birkenhead and others. Essentially, what Collins was pointing to was the cultural differences between the two sides that appeared, at that stage of the proceedings at least, to constitute an unbridgeable gap between them. These cultural differences, if they are not recognized, acknowledged and handled effectively, can very easily lead to miscommunication, misunderstanding and potential disaster in high stakes interactions such as these.

While the stakes may not be so high in our day-to-day business dealings, when we develop supply chain relationships with other organizations, whether long or short term, we encounter these cultural divides very frequently. When those supply chain relationships straddle international and linguistic borders, the cultural divide is magnified by distance, language, laws and customs. These are some of the diverse elements that make up the culture of a place, or an organization, and shape the beliefs and the behaviour of the people therein.

What is culture for?

In his book, *Wired for Culture: The natural history of human cooperation*, Mark Pagel (2012) describes culture as the innovation that has enabled Homo sapiens as a species to spread across the globe and adapt successfully in many different environments, climates and terrains. Clearly, it has been a highly successful innovation and as a species while we have an astonishing capacity to take on a bewildering diversity of cultures, as individuals we are generally very highly invested with the culture or cultures that we happen to belong to in our nation, our family and our place of work. Alan Weiss, author of a multitude of books on the business of consulting, describes culture as metaphoric DNA or the set of beliefs that governs behaviour (Weiss and Khan, 2009). Consequently, culture tends to be self-reinforcing through the behaviours that it shapes and can therefore be very stable over time and difficult to change. Culture therefore gives shape, stability and predictability to our world, allows us to take certain things for granted with regard to how people respond to certain cues, how they will behave in certain situations and how we can reasonably expect them to react under given sets of circumstances. Indeed, so pervasive is the culture that we are immersed in, that we can very easily be unaware of it at a conscious level. It is only when we bump up against a different culture that we realize that these things cannot be taken for granted in all place and at all times. Sometimes the result is culture shock. The ability to recognize culture shock for what it is and to be flexible in response are both increasingly valuable traits in life and in business in a world that is increasingly interconnected.

Culture shock

By way of example, I will tell you my own story of when I encountered culture shock in my early twenties when, back in the mid-80s, I left my home in Ireland and went to live in Spain. Initially I worked with other Anglophone expats like myself from Ireland, the UK, the US and Canada, and I was insulated from the local culture to a significant degree, particularly as I did not speak Spanish at the time. However, as I began to learn the language and I started to immerse myself more and more in the local way of life, I quickly realized that many things were very different from home and some of them, frankly, took a lot of getting used to. The first thing I noticed was that people spoke louder in almost all circumstances and often all at once. If you wanted to be part of the conversation you really needed to speak up and look confident with it; there was no place for shrinking violets. In fact, sometimes so boisterous were the exchanges between people to my ears that I would confuse friendly banter between two Spaniards with a full-blown argument. In fact, it seemed the threshold of tolerance for noise of all types was much, much higher than at home in relation to speech, traffic and music in public places – particularly at fiesta time. It was a result, I assumed, of apartment living in densely packed cities with narrow streets, as opposed to the three-bedroomed semi with garden back and front that was typical back home. The boundaries of personal space were different too. People would bump into you indoors and outdoors and not even acknowledge it or excuse themselves – they often wouldn't have even noticed. There was always lots of kissing and handshaking whenever you met somebody or said goodbye, whereas in Ireland a simple nod, or a wave or a short 'see you' would do the job just fine. A crowd of friends saying goodbye to each other at the end of an evening could take forever. The structure of the day was also very different. Breakfast was a non-event; lunch, very late, sometimes as late as 3 pm, was copious and long; and dinner, extremely late at 9 pm or even 10 pm meant that bedtime was pushed into the wee hours. Prime time TV shows on Spanish TV often don't end until 1 am! On many occasions in the early days when out with my new Spanish friends I would fall asleep after dinner in a bar or discotheque, much to their mirth and amusement. And yet, the more time went on, the more integrated I became into the milieu of Spanish life, the less I began to notice the differences. Eventually, I went to work in an all-Spanish firm, I learned the language and I met and married my Spanish wife. All in all I lived and worked in Spain for 10 years and to all intents and purposes,

I pretty much became a Spaniard culturally, taking on a lot of the assumptions, beliefs, perspectives and ultimately behaviours of the culture that I had immersed myself in for so long.

Cultural adaptability

When I eventually returned to live in Ireland with my Spanish wife and son, I experienced a reverse culture shock as we tried to adjust, or in my case readjust, to the cultural beliefs and assumptions that shape behaviour in Ireland day-to-day at work and in life in general. I relate this story to highlight the point that, while culture can be all pervasive and all consuming, culture is not nature. We can choose to adapt, to be flexible, to 'take on' new cultures or elements of cultures to forge new relationships and understandings with people from other cultural backgrounds for mutual benefit. I don't regard this as giving up, jettisoning or devaluing our original culture but rather adding to it, and becoming culturally more layered, competent and flexible. This type of adaptability, I believe, will be an ever more essential capability and skill within companies that must forge and maintain strong supply chain relationships with partner organizations, public and private, across the world. As I argued earlier, in a world of globalized working in which we depend for our success on the quality of our relationships with people in multiple organizations in many different countries, our innate attachment to our own culture may become an inadvertent barrier to our own success. We don't need to abandon our own cultural identity to sustain successful supply chain relationships but we do need to learn to be flexible and to build trust and rapport with people who belong to cultures other than our own.

Returning to Mark Pagel's book *Wired for Culture: The natural history of human cooperation* (2012), in the Preface Pagel tells the story of Dido a tribesman of the Gabbra, a tribe of nomadic pastoralists from the Horn of Africa. Pagel discovered that Dido, as well as English and his own native Gabbra language, could speak four other languages – Swahili, the trade language used all over East Africa, as well as the languages of three other nomadic pastoralist tribes from the same area, Rendille, Samburu and Turkana. When Pagel asked Dido why he could speak the languages of the other tribes, Dido replied 'So I can talk to them'. Dido clearly understood that it was in his own best interest to be flexible, adaptable and aware of the linguistic and cultural differences around him to the extent that he could communicate in six different languages. For most of us in business today, we may not need to become multilingual to be successful, but we do need to take a leaf from the book of Dido, the Gabbra tribesman, and realize that cultural awareness and adaptability is in our own best interest and can be the route to many business advantages that would otherwise remain out of reach for us.

Business relevance

If we want our businesses to thrive in supply chains made up of multiple organizations in different countries with whom we must work with every day to satisfy the requirements of our customers, then we urgently need to have people in our team who can do this effectively and consistently. If we can achieve cultural awareness, understanding and flexibility in a practical sense we will have developed a business capability that can be leveraged as a competitive advantage to ensure that our business will thrive in the face of competition. By cultural awareness, I refer to the sensitivity at a visceral level, that allows you to know that you are bumping up against a cultural difference when conducting a business activity, whether negotiating a sale, the release of a shipment through customs in a foreign port, or the signing of a contract to establish a joint venture enterprise with a partner from another country, expecting others to automatically conform to our own cultural norms and expectations and then getting all bent out of shape when they do not, is not only insensitive and rude, it can be bad for business, very bad. From awareness comes understanding and from understanding comes practical action that will produce the desired results. This is not something that can be left to chance. It requires purposeful preparation including research, study and training. For example, the *New York Times* reported that the US Secretary of Defence, James Mattis, stated shortly after his appointment that he wanted the Defence Department's regional desks at the Pentagon to be able to think the way the people in their respective countries would think and to really understand the countries and not just the issues that affect relations with the United States (NYT, 2016). Of course, we do not all have the resources of the US Department of Defence but if we are doing business with organizations in overseas locations, it is in our own best interest to take the trouble to inform ourselves about the context in which the people we are dealing with live and work. Many easily accessible resources are available on the internet as well as a plethora of books and publications related to the cultural aspects of doing business overseas.

Over the last 10 years I have done business personally, on the ground, in a wide range of locations around the world including China, India, UAE, Egypt, Malta, Spain, Croatia, the UK, the US, Puerto Rico, Mexico and Uruguay. During the same period, here in Ireland, both society in general and the workplace have become more diverse and I have worked and interacted actively with people from countries such as Poland, Lithuania, Nepal, Colombia, Costa Rica, Argentina and many more. These days, this is not at all uncommon in many countries in the developed world and it is something that more and more of us experience on a regular basis. While it is no doubt true that there is an emergent global business culture and that English has become the new business lingua franca, and that this facilitates trans-actional business dealings at a certain level and to a certain point, people do still possess their own individual cultural depth behind the veneer of the cosmopolitan business person, diplomat or official that you see in front of you. Being well informed about the world in general, possessing knowledge about the country and culture of your interlocutor and having a genuine interest in these matters can be extremely valuable when the purpose, requirement and need of the interaction moves beyond the purely transactional, and requires longer-term collaboration, deeper levels of partnership, teamwork or gain sharing. All of these are increasingly important features of the types of business dealings required to sustain modern-day supply chain relationships. This challenge is greatest for small- and medium-sized enterprises (SMEs) for various reasons. Firstly, large multinational corporations are able to project their own cultures, often anglophone by default or by design, to a much greater degree into their global operations and among the people they employ abroad as well as among the companies that they chose to do business with. In these global production networks, people are more likely to be familiar with, and to be trained in, this emerging global anglophone business culture. SMEs, on the other hand, will often be looking to deal with companies in overseas locations that are not unlike themselves in terms of scale and resources. Consequently, it is much more likely that they will bump up against cultural barriers sooner and will have less experience, familiarity and resources available to help them overcome these challenges.

In a recent project that I was involved in, the objective was to develop and implement an international supply chain solution for a business based in Ireland that wished to distribute a fresh food product into the Spanish multiple retail market. Both companies were SMEs of comparable size and turnover. Because of the nature of the product, particularly the requirements to keep it in optimum conditions of quality and freshness during transport from Ireland to Spain, together with the fragmented structure of the fresh food wholesale and retail supply chain within Spain, the preferred solution, and the one that would provide the greatest scope for sustainable and profitable business in the future, was to set up a joint venture company in Spain between the Irish exporting company and a Spanish wholesale company that would ideally have well-established retail business connections and distributions networks in the country already. Various potential joint-venture candidates were considered and one, which met the requirements for size, capability, market knowledge and distribution network, was selected to pursue negotiations to commence activities that would lead in due course to a joint venture arrangement through a step-by-step process, initially with transactional sale and purchase, followed by joint investment with profit sharing and finally the establishment of the joint venture enterprise with shared ownership. In moving along that continuum, some of the challenges, rooted in both the national and organizational cultures of the two enterprises that were encountered included the following:

- speed of decision-making and accountability for the implementation of agreed actions
- responsiveness to requests and communication needs

- familiarity and competence in the use of information and communications technologies
- language proficiency of key people and decision-makers – one challenge was that the CEO of the Irish company did not speak Spanish and the CEO of the Spanish company did not speak English
- locus of decision-making within the management hierarchy and the degree of delegation of the power of decision from higher to lower levels of management
- need and requirement for formal, legally binding agreements at different points along the development of the relationship
- attitude to risk in general and to the sharing of risk and reward in particular
- value placed on resource contribution of different types such as time, money, land, equipment, material resource and management know-how.

In this complex mix of different national cultures, organizational cultures, communications barriers and personal styles, it is easy to see the potential for misunderstanding and the difficulties in building mutual trust and empathy can be heightened and amplified.

A practical framework for building international business relationships

Building trust and rapport

Working through this kind of process can be frustrating, time-consuming and costly. It is pretty much a given that developing a business relationship, whether a simple buy and sell relationship, a distributor–principal relationship or a joint-venture relationship is going to take longer and cost more with a company in a foreign jurisdiction, than it would with a company in your home jurisdiction. So how might you, as a business owner or manager, maximize the probability of success and stack the deck in your favour as you embark on establishing sustainable and mutually beneficial supply chain relationships with other organizations across international borders? As with most endeavours in business, it pays to be well prepared, to have your homework done in advance and to have a structured process to guide you through the steps.

Prepare in advance

When considering an overseas market and territory and how best to approach the challenges of doing business there, it is important to be well informed about the local business operating regime. Valuable information can be gleaned from the internet and from publications regarding the economy, demographics and infrastructure. Embassies, state and regional commercial and development agencies, both those of your own country and those of the countries of interest, can provide very valuable help and support in relation to legal, fiscal and governance arrangements and may also be able to provide practical help in terms of trade missions, connection to channel partners, the provision of office space and business services or even financial incentives in certain circumstances.

Allocate sufficient time and resources

When reviewing the journey that business people have travelled to set up, consolidate and maintain successful international supply chain relationships, what they invariably report is that the process took far longer than they ever would have imagined at the outset and required the commitment of more resources than they would have anticipated. It is important to plan for this in a realistic way and to understand early on that the endeavour is going to require sustained effort and commitment over a significant period of time. Planning in advance and being realistic will both help to ensure that the resources are made available and increase the probability that the initiative is carried through to successful finalization.

Be prepared to travel

As well as the commitment of time and resource it is important to realize that there is no substitute for travelling to the target areas and for meeting the people you are looking to do business with face to face, conversing with them, getting to know them and appreciating the context in which they live and work. No amount of internet research, background reading, telephone or video conferencing is going to substitute for the richness and complexity of the intense learning experience of being in place, on the ground, face to face with your interlocutors. Quite simply, if you are not willing travel to build personal ties to the place and the people, you are not going to be successful in building successful and sustainable international supply chain relationships. Depending on the type of business relationship, this may be an ongoing, periodic requirement that requires a particular mindset and skill set to leverage to its maximum potential.

Invest in people and skills

A look at the course offerings of some of the top business schools in the world today, such as the London Business School, INSEAD, Harvard Business School and MIT Sloan, illustrates the growing emphasis and appreciation of the need for specific skills development in the areas of international and global business management and leadership and schools and universities all across the world have now developed specific offerings to cater for the ever growing requirements in this space to create business professionals who possess the awareness, flexibility and cultural intelligence to help their businesses thrive in an international and global context. English today has become the pre-eminent international business language. There are some 375 million native speakers and a total of 1.5 billion people in the world who can communicate competently in English – that is about 20 per cent of the world's population (Lyons, 2017). Some multinational business organizations such as Airbus, Nokia and Samsung, which do not have their origins in English-speaking countries, have even adopted English as their internal official corporate language to facilitate communication and coordination across their geographically dispersed operations.

Notwithstanding, the emergence of English as the lingua franca of global business, it is still common when working overseas outside the multinational sector to find that competence in business English is patchy. Likewise, if your operations involve an element of direct business-to business, or business-to-consumer customer service in an overseas market, the interactions will not be in English but rather in the local language. Consequently, as SMEs progress in the internationalization of their business and supply chains, particularly when they are looking to sell and promote their products and services overseas, competence in a range of international languages will become essential and will open access to a whole range of new customers and business relationships. Depending on the area of interest and the type of business relationships that you need to develop, hiring or developing skills in languages such as Spanish, Portuguese, French, German, Russian or Mandarin Chinese may need to form part of your investment and development strategy.

Think of the process in a holistic way

It is important to think of the endeavour as part of a holistic business development strategy and to understand how the various initiatives impinge on and affect each other. Having clearly defined business objectives, understanding what the achievement of those objectives will mean for the business, and putting in place effective metrics and measures that indicate progress towards achieving those objectives will go a long way to ensuring that you view and understand the process of developing this international supply chain relationships as an integral part of the overall business strategy.

Expect unforeseen challenges to arise

It is important to manage both your own expectations and the expectations of other colleagues, peers, managers and reports. There will be ups and downs, and sometimes it will appear that things are progressing frustratingly slowly. There may be occasions when you find that you have put a lot of time and effort into building a relationship and the final deal cannot be consummated. These setbacks can be disheartening at the time, but they can be invaluable learning experiences that will set you up for success next time provided that you do not give up and abandon the endeavour as a result of these setbacks. The best way to avoid the danger of giving up is to expect that there will be setbacks and to plan contingency actions and measures in the event that these risks materialize. If you have provision for them, then they will not faze you. If they do not occur, it will be a bonus and you will have the satisfaction of having been prudent and pragmatic.

'I see the light in you' – the personal touch

In India and Nepal, the most respectful salutation that you can receive from another person is the joining together of the hands with a slight bowing of the head while saying the word 'Namaste', meaning 'I see the light in you'. This respectful acknowledgement of the validity and presence of the other is the essence of the spirit that underpins effective cultural flexibility in business, the ability to look, see and understand what is in the other person when negotiating any kind of business transaction, cooperation or partnership. While the pervading international business culture today may well be one that is modulated through the medium of English and the approaches and methodologies of doing business that have been developed over many decades in Europe and North America, if you can push beyond this surface level and tap into the cultural context of the people that you are dealing with in a genuine and sincere manner with interest and curiosity, not only will you enjoy a profoundly more layered, complex and personally satisfying experience, but you may well establish lifelong contacts and friends and do very well in your business dealings as well.

By way of example, my own brother, who has been doing business in China for over two decades, explained some aspects of this to me in a recent conversation. He explained that a cultural aspect of Chinese business that he has found again and again is that Chinese business dealings are very social. As he puts it: 'They like to meet you in person. They want to be your friend. They want to take you to dinner. But you can only do this by meeting them. You can do a lot of business in China via email or phone, but it is only by visiting them that you can build up a personal relationship, which builds up trust over time. When you have their trust you can look to enhance your trading terms on both cost and, more importantly, on payment terms. Eliminating deposits and getting to open credit can only be done by putting in the legwork to visit them in China and socialize.' He explains further, 'In response to a business request in China, an inexperienced European or American may think upon hearing the reply "no problem" that everything is well, and everything will be fine. When I hear "no problem", I start to worry. At that point I will look further into the subject and ask more probing questions. What you will often discover is that they don't currently do what you are asking for. They would like to do it in the future and they don't like to let you down or give negative feedback. You need to probe deeply a "no problem" answer so you can make an informed decision regarding the real status and avoid delays or missed deadlines, which can be very frustrating and potentially very costly.'

Summary

In this chapter we have explored the concept of culture as it applies to international business interactions with the full range of supply chain players such as suppliers, customers, service providers and strategic business partners of all types. Culture, although a complex concept can be expressed succinctly for practical purposes as suggested by Alan Weiss as the set of beliefs that governs behaviour (Weiss and Khan, 2009) or as I put it 'the way we do things around here'. We have seen that international cultural barriers can be an obstacle to business success when dealing overseas, slowing progress towards the achievement of business objectives, producing frustration, misunderstanding and resource wastage in the form of time, effort and money. In the early days of Jollibee Food Corporation's expansion from its home base in the Philippines to other Asian markets this was an experience that was all too familiar until they grappled with the challenges in an open and creative way before progressing to ultimate success (Bartlett and Beamish, 2014). On the other hand, we have also seen that cultural awareness and acuity is a key competitive advantage in international business that can and does enable businesses to achieve speed, flexibility and agility in their dealings with international supply chain partners and tap into opportunities that are unattainable or simply invisible to their less culturally attuned competitors.

Several further key points are noteworthy:

- Culture is pervasive and very stable over time and most people are highly invested in the cultures they belong to.

- Being culturally aware and adaptive provides significant business benefits in international business dealings in delivering business benefits such as speed to market, enhanced customer service, increased sales and higher profitability.

- The skill sets required to be successful in international business dealings can be learned and internalized in the business provided the requisite focus, resource and commitment is brought to bear.

- These skill sets comprise both hard skills related to legal, regulatory and fiscal requirements as well as soft skills related to customs, traditions, taboos and communications cues.

- Preparation, resources, physical presence and a long-term approach are critical ingredients for success in international business dealings.

References

Bartlett, CA and Beamish, PW (2014) *Transnational Management: Text, cases and readings in cross border management*, McGraw Hill, Singapore, pp 26–45

Lyons, D (2017) How Many People Speak English and Where is it Spoken, 7/17. Available from www.babbel.com/en/magazine/how-many-people-speak-english-and-where-is-it-spoken/ [last accessed 16 August 2017]

Pagel, MD (2012) *Wired for Culture: The Natural History of Human Cooperation*, Penguin, London

The Editorial Board, NYT (2016) An Experienced Choice for the Pentagon, 12/16. Available from www.nytimes.com/2016/12/02/opinion/an-experienced-leader-for-the-pentagon.html [last accessed 14 July 2017]

Weiss, A and Khan, O (2009) *The Global Consultant: How to make seven figures across borders*, Wiley, Singapore

We're getting hitched

04

Long-term inter-organizational relationships

Not all relationships are created equal and in business, asymmetrical power balances between supplier and customer and between different partners in strategic alliances are more the norm than the exception. On both sides of the power balance, there are challenges to be overcome to ensure a successful relationship that delivers business benefits for all parties. The key questions of common objectives, shared benefits and agreed-upon metrics are crucial for the long-term sustainability of supply chain business relationships and we are going to explore these key concepts in this chapter.

Transformation of the global economy

To set the scene for why the quality of these relationships is becoming ever more important for sustained business success and competitive advantage it is important to be cognizant of the fact that we are living through a tremendous transformation of the world economy that has been ongoing for many decades, which is giving rise to the need for companies to cultivate multiple working relationships in new and complex ways across international borders with suppliers, service providers, state agencies and communities. The reasons for the transformation in the world economy and the mechanisms by which these changes are taking place are the subjects of intense political and academic debate and not a little controversy. The various proponents and detractors of economic globalization all put forward their views and opinions as to how, why or whether these changes are desirable and at different times over the past 70 years or so, the pace and emphasis of these transformations has ebbed and flowed as opinions and policies have shifted in one direction and then another. No doubt this pattern will continue into the future. Whereas at the time of writing in 2018 we are at a point where economic globalization may appear to be in retreat as the full panoply of consequences of the economic crash of 2008 continue to play out, one way or another, the process has progressed to such a degree, facilitated by technological and regulatory change, that businesses will continue to be faced with the challenges of forging strong, sustainable working relationships with new and unfamiliar partners in order to develop. Therefore, regardless of the rights and wrongs, or what various parties consider should or shouldn't be, this is the reality that we inhabit, right now, at this moment in time, and consequently businesses must adapt and negotiate their way through these unfolding changes in pragmatic ways to ensure that they can continue to grow and thrive in the future, satisfy the needs of their customers, and secure the livelihoods of their shareholders and employees whatever way events unfold in the future.

Multinationals and global networks

Multinational corporations have led the way and have developed networks of production that stretch across the globe. They have done this to maximize their ability to service their customers in markets worldwide, exploit greater opportunities for growth, maximize their profitability and increase their business value. In doing this they have carried with them their suppliers and service providers who have had to develop the capabilities and capacities to follow their multinational customers across the globe. Meanwhile, the same factors that have facilitated the global spread of multinational companies' economic activities from more developed to less developed economies have also opened the home markets of these same companies in the developed economies to competition from abroad. The implications of this is that in many sectors and markets it is increasingly difficult to grow and thrive by concentrating all vertical activities from procurement through to sales within home markets. For example, from the 1970s there has been a displacement of low value-added manufacturing from the US and Europe to lower wage locations in Latin America, Eastern Europe and East and Southeast Asia. Meanwhile higher value planning, design, R&D and high-end manufacturing has concentrated in the core economies of North America and Europe. This ongoing process is compelling even small- and medium-sized companies that may not, a priori, have an international vocation or ambition, to venture into global competition whether they like it or not. In many cases they are not very well prepared and if they cannot respond adequately they run the serious risk of being overtaken by newcomers from outside or indeed by existing home-market competitors better equipped to leverage the opportunities of global competition.

Inter-organizational relationships

There are myriad ways in which companies can configure their operations to compete in this internationalized economy depending on the sector, the products and services they provide and the opposing pressures for global standardization and local responsiveness that they experience. Some adopt more centralized strategies holding value creation at the core in their home markets, while carrying out production and assembly in overseas markets. Others adopt strategies whereby they become truly transnational with more competences and capabilities devolved to international business units where local responsiveness is important. Additionally, we hear about tools and tactics such as offshoring, outsourcing and global procurement in relation to how enterprises adapt to global threats and opportunities. These different strategies and approaches have one thing in common. They are leading to a multiplicity of new and complex inter-organizational relationships. In many cases, these are relationships with new and unfamiliar entities, such as government agencies in foreign countries, civic communities, consumer groups and NGOs, as well as with myriad suppliers and service providers spread across many countries with different national and business cultures operating in jurisdictions with different governance rules, regulations and legal frameworks. Some of these relationships are situational and short term and are required to respond to specific short-term needs such as building a production facility in an overseas location whereas others may be required to become long-term stable relationships and a key part and contributor to the competitive advantage of the organization. Relationships with key suppliers of critical materials and services would fall into the second category. Inter-organizational relationships encounter many challenges, and yet are crucial to the continued success of more and more businesses for reasons that we have already outlined. As business evolves and fragments into myriad specialities, as firms push ever more to a focus on core competences the requirement to be able to successfully cooperate, collaborate and to form partnerships is becoming ever more a key competence and a differentiator between competitors.

The importance of clear objectives

The difficulties encountered in forming and sustaining successful inter-organizational relationships generally revolve around issues related to clarity on objectives, measures and value (Weiss, 2002). Often, the objectives of the relationship are not made explicit and as a consequence are assumed implicitly to be default on the part of the cooperating parties. The trouble is these assumed objectives are often in opposition to each other and inevitably become the source of friction, strife and dissatisfaction.

An example of a long-term inter-organizational relationship: a pharmaceutical manufacturer and a logistics service provider

This is an example of a manufacturer of consumer pharmaceutical products that has developed a long-term working relationship with a provider of logistics services for the warehousing and shipping of finished product. From the manufacturer's point of view, this is desirable, because it allows finished product to be moved out of the production plant while quality approval takes place, thus freeing up valuable space within the plant that can be dedicated to other value-added activities such as manufacturing or packaging lines, R&D, laboratories and so on rather than to warehousing. Additionally, this arrangement simplifies the process of despatch at the plant. The product can be loaded onto trailers as it comes off the lines without the need to consolidate and sort by order, batch or customer. These tasks can be carried out later, at the offsite warehouse operated by the logistics service provider, after the quality department approves and releases the product for shipping. From the manufacturer's point of view, the advantages include the better use of plant facilities, savings in labour costs through simplification and the avoidance of investing valuable capital in warehouse buildings, equipment and technology. From the logistics service providers' point of view the chief benefit is the income stream, which provides for the amortization of the investment already made in warehousing and transport infrastructure, systems and personnel and the profit generated by exploiting the economies of scale and process efficiencies that the logistics service provider can provide to the manufacturer. Generally, the charging mechanism in a traditional logistics outsourcing arrangement like this would be built around charge rates for pallet storage per week or month, rates for handling pallets in and out of the offsite warehouse and rates for the transfer of trailer loads between the manufacturing plant and the off-site warehouse facilities operated by the service provider.

Self-interest of the parties

Often, the ostensible objectives for the arrangement are expressed in terms of how many pallets will be stored on average, how frequently they will move and what the times of operation will be. The logistics service provider will calculate the rates to be charged as a function of these parameters and these will generally be at a level that provides a reasonable profit margin to the service provider, while at the same time being affordable and competitive from the manufacturer's point of view in terms of the wider business advantages that are being achieved in terms of space saving, capital expenditure avoidance and reduction in complexity. However, this format is problematic and short sighted because it sets the self-interest of the manufacturer and that of the service provider in conflict with each other from the outset, and it fails to identify and explicitly express what the true objectives of the relationship are. This will inevitably lead to tension and friction, and an inability of the partners to take full advantage of the potential benefits of the working relationship. For example, if the quality department of the manufacturer introduces a new process that speeds up the rate of approval and release of products for shipping, the stock will turn faster through the outside warehouse and the average stock holding will drop. This will have the effect of decreasing the logistics provider's revenue stream for storage on the same overall throughput of stock. So, what is beneficial to the manufacturer, that is, getting product released and out to market sooner, is detrimental to the logistics service provider, who may begin to lose margin due to the fixed overhead component of costs and may begin to agitate with the manufacturer for a storage rate increase to compensate. In effect, the arrangement masked the conflicting underlying objectives of the two parties. Any kind of improvement initiated by the manufacturer to increase stock turns or reduce inventory will be detrimental to the logistics services partner.

In other cases, these outsourced logistics services are charged on a cost plus margin or management fee basis, with the margin or fee being a percentage of the cost. Perversely then, the higher the cost, the better off the service provider is and the worse off the manufacturer is. Again the underlying objectives of the two parties are at cross purposes. In outsourced warehousing, for example, there is always scope for process improvement resulting in higher productivity and lower unit costs through changes in the structure of work, planning, communication, equipment and technology. However, a charging mechanism that ensures that the logistics service provider will be worse off if it introduces such productivity gains is simply not fit for purpose. These arrangements are made in good faith on the part of both parties, albeit with lack of real insight into the potential of the arrangement and the opportunities for exploiting mutual business benefits, and often the parties are surprised and disappointed when the relationship tenses and sours over the duration of the term of the contract. The manufacturer is disappointed because the service provider did not bring new ideas and innovation to the table as the supposed expert in the field of logistics and the service provider is disappointed because the volumes and margins did not turn out as projected in the original costing exercise that underpinned their initial proposals. In many instances, the contracts are not renewed at the end of the term and the pattern is repeated with a new outsourced partner in much the same manner.

Make objectives explicit and aligned

To avoid this kind of thing, it is important to make the underlying business objectives explicit from the start of the engagement and then to work very carefully to align them in such a way that the self-interest of both the manufacturing outsourcer and the logistics service provider are oriented in the same direction. This may add time and complexity to the proposal and to the contracting phase of the project but when considered in terms of the return on investment over the lifetime of the contract, it is easily justifiable. What is perhaps more challenging in the face of the traditional way of approaching these inter-organizational relationships is that it requires greater openness and trust than would be customary. Consequently, the skills associated with developing and building frank, open and trustful working relationships become ever more valuable at the interfaces between the partners. Trust will only be established when the first party is confident that the second party is operating with the first's best interest at heart and vice versa, in the firm knowledge and conviction that both will be better as a result.

By way of example of how this has been achieved in practice among cutting-edge companies, let's look at an example of an international manufacturer of a range of consumer food products who required to contract with a logistics service provider to receive and store finished product, pick and pack orders for distribution to wholesalers, large multiple retailers and smaller retailers in a regional market, and execute the delivery of orders to all customers. The proposal and contract negotiations were based firmly around the clear and explicit understanding of the objectives, measures and value of the engagement. By 'objectives', we mean a clear expression of the business-relevant outcomes to be achieved. By 'measures' we mean those metrics that will indicate the mutual progress towards achieving those objectives, and by 'value' we mean the business benefits that are provided by reaching those objectives. Typically, in an engagement of this type, the manufacturer is looking to achieve a range of different business outcomes that will include such things as:

- avoidance of capital expenditure in non-core infrastructure, equipment and personnel for logistics activities such as warehousing and transport;
- access to best-in-class knowledge and innovation in logistics practice to drive efficiency in operation and improved service in fulfilment;
- access to economies of scale to deliver operational cost savings on warehousing, transport and distribution; and
- reduced specific inventory to support the business and to liberate working capital.

Likewise, the logistics service provider is typically looking at a set of desired business outcomes that include some of the following:

- a predictable revenue stream for an extended period
- contribution to operational costs
- amortization of capital investments in buildings, equipment and systems
- generation of profit
- experience and exposure to industry sector requirements and standards
- positive references from reputable and satisfied customers.

If these two sets of objectives are brought to the surface in an explicit manner at the outset of the engagement, they can be explored for mutual alignment. In this specific example of engagement between the manufacturer and the logistics service provider we were working with the manufacturer. We had determined that because of the large batch sizes, a considerable proportion of the manufacturer's stock profile was suited to a type of racking called push-back racking storing pallets four deep as opposed to conventional pallet racking which stores pallets just one deep. The advantages from the manufacturer's point of view included that the total cubic space and footprint of the building required to hold the stock would be smaller, consequently travel distances for the put away and retrieval of stock would be shorter, favouring more efficient stock replenishment to order picking locations and shorter overall order picking routes. This all translates into less space, reduced travel time, fewer people and ultimately lower costs and lower rates for storage, handling and order picking. However, traditionally most logistics service providers favour conventional racking layouts in their facilities. This is because many logistics contracts are short, in the range of one to three years, and these facilities must accommodate different contracts, with different stock profiles and different operational requirements over their lifetime of perhaps 15 to 20 years. Specialized racking systems such as push-back racks, can be four to six times more expensive per pallet position than conventional pallet racking and consequently it is difficult for the logistics service provider to amortize the investment with a short-term contract, particularly when they may find the system unsuited to the next contract that comes into the facility.

Armed with this knowledge, the two parties were able to negotiate in an informed and frank manner. The manufacturer wanted lower rates over an extended period and the logistics provider wanted a predictable revenue stream for as long as possible. Both were able to align their objectives by establishing a contract for a duration far longer than current industry norms that provided the logistics service provider with a predictable revenue stream over a period sufficiently long to be able to amortize the investment in specialist equipment and at the same time to provide very competitive rates to the manufacturer. Of course, there were other measures agreed to ensure that the productivity, quality standards and ongoing process improvements would be an integral part of the arrangements to ensure that expectations would be met during the lifetime of the agreement. In the same manner, creative examination of the potential to align each party's explicit objectives will give rise to very beneficial and sometimes unexpected arrangements whereby the relationship can be built on solid foundations that ensure that when one party does well the other does well also. This lays the foundation for sustainable long-term relationships, where trust can be built up over time between the parties, and their best interests are aligned. In our example, the manufacturer knows that it is getting the best deal in terms of service, price and quality, and the service provider has a guarantee of long-term revenue stability.

Relevant metrics to measure progress towards achieving the objectives

Of course, there is little point in setting objectives that cannot be measured. How else will we know whether we are making progress towards the objective, whether we have reached the objective or whether we have exceeded the objective. To be useful, metrics must be truly indicative of the objective that is of interest, they must be straightforward, and they must be easy to compute and understand. They must provide real insight to those who will use them to guide their actions in making progress towards the objectives, otherwise they can be less than useless and serve only as a distraction, an inappropriate use of resource, or worse, they may drive actions that move the relationship away from the true best interests of both parties. Well-chosen metrics and measures are the cornerstone of all successful inter-organizational relationships that are grounded in mutually beneficial objectives. To do this, they need to be specified and chosen very carefully, a task that requires trust, focused attention and clarity of purpose.

A quantitative metric to compare global warehouse productivity

I have come across many situations in which a plethora of metrics are computed and reported upon on a regular basis but where these metrics bear little relation to the real business objectives or they are not specified with true insight into the nature of the process being measured. In another case that I was involved with, a manufacturer with production operations in several countries on different continents whose supply chain director was interested in comparing the productivity of the picking and shipping operations at the finished goods warehouses of the various plants with a view to cross-pollinating best practices across the international network and increasing overall productivity across the global network. The finished goods warehouses at the production plants despatched product internationally to another vertical tier within the same organization as well as to third parties who used the finished product as an input to their own production process to produce the final consumer-ready product. The metric chosen had the virtue of simplicity, that is, pallets picked and shipped per man-hour; however it didn't take account of the operational differences between warehouse operations at the various plants thus giving a misreading of which plants were more productive and which were less productive. In inter-organizational relationships the simplistic specification of metrics in this way can lead to frustration, mistrust and can call the entire measurement system into disrepute and undermining the ability of organizations to achieve their objectives.

In this case, the difficulty was that whereas some plants predominantly made and shipped large volume products for big markets, others had a more complex mix of lower consumption products for smaller national markets. Consequently, the former picked and shipped a higher proportion of full pallets. These can be picked and moved to the shipping bays in one single operation using a forklift truck, whereas the latter required the manual picking of a mix of different items onto pallets that subsequently required checking, wrapping and labelling, which is clearly a far more labour-intensive process. In a situation like this, direct comparison cannot be made between the productivity of the plants based on this metric as it was being specified and calculated. To overcome this limitation, either an adjustment factor could be introduced to enable the productivity of the plants to be compared to each other, or perhaps more usefully, each plant could develop an agreed standard for its own process. Each plant could measure itself against its own standard and the performance with respect to the standards could then be compared directly between the various plants. This is an example of a situation in which the metric is a quantitative measure and can be calculated mathematically based on data that are collected from the records of movements and transactions within the warehouse operation. Not all metrics need to be quantitative to be useful, however. Consider, for example, a metric designed to measure the effectiveness of inter-organizational communication between those working at the interface between two collaborating organizations. This metric is important because it is an indicator of the quality and sustainability of the working relationship. A metric like this could be defined in terms of distinctions in the subjective experience of the associates in the two collaborating organizations.

A qualitative metric to measure international communications effectiveness

In a real-life example between a producer of a fresh food product in northern Europe and a distributor of the product in the markets of a southern European country, the day-to-day interaction of the associates in each company included the negotiation and clarification of price and of product availability, which varied greatly on a week-to-week basis, as well as confirmation of order quantities, product mix, timing of deliveries, and the confirmation of deliveries and payments. Given that the associates were interacting in a fast-paced, dynamic environment, using a lingua franca, English, of which none of them was a native speaker, and each company operated its own distinct corporate culture as well as different national cultures it was important for the sustainability of the mutual arrangements to measure how effective the inter-organizational communication was on an ongoing basis.

To do this a short questionnaire was designed that could be administered in a matter of minutes that allowed the key components of responsiveness, clarity and trust to be measured on a regular basis. In the early days of the relationship, the southern Europeans learned that if they provided the northern Europeans with specific timings for their next actions, as opposed to indicating more ambiguously 'as soon as possible', they received far fewer follow-up queries and interruptions from their northern European interlocutors. Conversely, the northern Europeans learned that the patterns of consumer shopping in southern European municipal markets and supermarkets where the shopper prefers to buy very fresh produce in small quantities every day, as opposed to one big weekly purchase, means that order confirmations necessarily come in later and are more complex in their make-up than is the norm in northern Europe. This helped the northern Europeans to design their fulfilment system to taking this reality into consideration rather than considering it some sort of laxity on the part of the southern European partner. This crucial learning helped to build trust and mutual respect between the partners, and laid the foundation for a sustainable working relationship with considerable benefits in terms of growth and profits accruing to both organizations over time.

The CRUDA metrics

Whether quantitative or qualitative, the requirements for a good metric can be remembered easily using the CRUDA acronym.

A good metric must be:

- Computable – it must be a metric that is expressed in terms of quantities that can be calculated in the case of tangible metrics that are quantitative in nature, or in terms of clear distinctions that can be readily expressed and perceived in the case metrics that are qualitative in nature.

- Relevant – it must be relevant to progress towards the achievement of the objective that it seeks to measure.

- Useable – it must have meaning for the managers and associates in their day-to-day work so that it can be used to guide their actions that they take to achieve the objectives of the business.

- Data must be accessible – the data and information that is required to compute the metric must be readily obtainable from systems, observation, surveys and so on and the effort required to collect the data and compute the metric must not outweigh the usefulness of the metric.

- Automated – the metric must be capable of being generated quickly and efficiently from the data inputs in an automated fashion using spreadsheets, macros, report writers or other tools that can process, calculate and present the metric in a readily digestible format.

The judicious choice of appropriate metrics that are simple and easy to understand yet not over simplistic or naïve, that capture the true essence of the process they are intended to measure, and that are aligned with the mutually agreed business objectives will go a long way to cementing the foundations of successful and sustainable inter-organizational relationships, whether they are between business units within a group, different businesses working together within a single national economy or those collaborating across international, cultural and linguistic borders.

What does it all mean for the business?

When clarifying objectives and developing the metrics that will allow progress towards those objectives to be measured, it is essential that these objectives be framed in terms of outcomes that deliver real business value to the parties and that objectives are truly aligned with the overarching strategies of the businesses that the relationship is designed to underpin. For example, an overemphasis on objectives aligned with cost control in a business aiming to deliver high-quality, highly differentiated services and products at premium rates may lead to service and quality failures that alienate customers and contradict the stated business strategy. Likewise, an overemphasis on service-related objectives in a business whose strategy is to be the cost leader in the market may lead to an erosion of margins that endanger the survival of the business over the long term. There needs to be a cogent and coherent connection between the strategy of the business and, the long-term inter-organizational relationship it chooses to enter with other entities and partners, and the objectives established for those relationships. Unfortunately, the reality is that this is not always what happens in practice due to the ineffective translation of business strategy into operational reality. This is most often the result of an absence of appropriate resource allocation, planning, investment, training and communication. Business strategy rarely fails in the formulation but rather more often in the execution (Weiss, 1994). Indeed, a middling quality strategy that is well executed will often deliver far greater business benefits than an excellently formulated strategy that is poorly executed. While this is an ever-present challenge within organizations, it is an even greater test of business acumen when it involves aligning strategies and objectives between two or more businesses working together to achieve mutually beneficial goals. While each organization may be pursuing a different strategy, each one needs to be fully aware and cognizant of how the relationship between them is going to underpin both their own strategy and that of their cooperating partner or partners. This requires a highly sophisticated level of understanding and communication within and between the key stakeholders in the partner companies.

What's your strategy? International sales of commoditized industrial products

Early in my career, I worked with a manufacturing company in Spain that designed, manufactured and distributed an industrial product worldwide. It was a product that had become commoditized in international markets and differentiated, for the most part, on price, availability and lead time. Global competition and the implementation of uniform design and manufacturing standards among all the major international players in the more developed markets had ensured that the quality, durability and flexibility of application of the product offerings of all the reputable suppliers had become uniform and ceased to be differentiating factors. One of the key success factors in securing contracts of supply was the ability to respond quickly to customer requests for quotations with prices, materials lists, technical drawings and a statement of lead times for manufacture, delivery and installation at the very beginning of the sales process. Rapid response to these requests for quotation dramatically raised the probability of being included in the selection shortlist of potential suppliers in the vendor selection process, which generally involved the customer pitting two or three of the major vendors against each other in a process centred primarily on price and ability to deliver on time. Any delay in the response to the initial request for quotation risked exclusion from the selection process and the loss of any chance to secure the contract to supply. In many instances the rapidity of response, was more important than the accuracy of the pricing at that early stage of the process, particularly in the Anglophone and Asian markets where the initial budget price is considered an opening position used to orient expectations and facilitate the creation of a shortlist of the most realistic offerings.

For overseas projects and installations in countries such as the UK, France, Germany, Israel, Hong Kong, Taiwan and others, the Spanish company used long-term, in-market alliances with local resellers and distributors of industrial products as the preferred route to market. The traditional model had been that a request for quotation that was received by a local reseller or distributor from a prospect in their country was filled out on a standard template by the local reseller and sent to the international department at the company headquarters in Spain. In the International Commercial Department, these requests for quotation had to be translated into Spanish for the technical department who prepared the quotations including prices, itemized lists of materials, technical drawings, statements of lead times for manufacture, delivery and installation, statements of materials qualities, finish, design and manufacturing standards and so on. Proprietary design programs and CAD applications were used to produce these comprehensive proposal documents. These outputs, in Spanish, were then sent back to the international commercial office to be translated into French, German or English, before being sent back to the distributor or reseller in the overseas markets who in turn processed the commercial aspect of the quotation further for delivery to the customer. This quotation process was a legacy of when the company had been one of the first manufacturers of this product in the Spanish market when it had been considered a quality supplier commanding a premium price. Over time, it became increasingly apparent that the overseas resellers were missing the train on many projects because the customers had pre-selected vendors and moved the process on to the next stage while the reseller was still waiting for a response from the office in Spain. The commoditization process had proceeded much further and more rapidly in the more developed overseas markets such as the UK and Germany where there had been many quality producers active for many years.

In effect, the inter-organizational relationships between the Spanish company and the resellers in relation to the setting of objectives, and the measures of success for quotation response times, communications protocols, conversion rates and sales had not been accounted for. The different strategic perspectives of each as a function of their differing market conditions and expectations had not been made clear and explicit so that both sides would have a common understanding of the requirements. The resellers were operating on a strategy of cost leadership in commoditized markets whereas the manufacturer believed it was operating on a strategy of product differentiation. Consequently, the Spanish company was becoming disappointed with the performance of the distributors and resellers in terms of conversion rates and sales and the resellers were becoming frustrated at losing sales opportunities due to the time it was taking the manufacturing company to respond with basic quotations to enable them to successfully get onto the shortlists for selection processes. Eventually, the Spanish manufacturing company learned the lesson and developed several computer applications that enabled different types of quotation to be produced more rapidly and output automatically in the main languages of the distributors, in English, French and German. In this way budget quotations could be produced rapidly, and basic technical drawings could be generated automatically. Furthermore, foreign resellers and distributors who had the resources and capability were then licensed and trained to use these programs themselves, thus eliminating the need to refer all quotations back to the central technical office in Spain, thereby dramatically increasing the local speed of response to quotation requests and the overall capacity of the global organization to produce quotations and more importantly, to convert sales.

Summary

In this chapter, we have seen how the key concepts of clear objectives, relevant metrics and alignment of value are the key ingredients for successful long-term, inter-organizational relationships that are mutually beneficial and sustainable. Several key points stand out:

- The globalization of the world economy has multiplied the opportunities and the need for firms to form multiple inter-organizational relationships internationally with suppliers, service providers, state agencies, communities and consumers to ensure that they can grow and thrive in the future.

- These inter-organizational relationships can be both short term and long term. Long-term inter-organizational relationships tend to be strategic in nature and need to be based clear objectives, relevant metrics and an alignment and shared understanding of the business value to be derived from the relationship.

- The objectives of inter-organizational relationships need to be made explicit and must be defined in terms that incentivize all parties towards mutually beneficial behaviours.

- Metrics must be indicative of progress towards the objectives that they are designed to measure. Additionally, they must be CRUDA, that is, **C**omputable, **R**elevant, **U**seable, **D**ata accessible, and **A**utomated.

- Clear metrics underpin the sustainability of inter-organizational relationships and help build trust, understanding and mutual respect between the cooperating parties.

- The business value that is expected to be derived from achieving the objectives of the relationship must be congruent with the business strategies of the cooperating parties.

- Explicit and aligned understanding of the business value to be obtained reinforces the relationships and ensures that focus is maintained on the benefits and competitive advantages delivered by the relationship.

References

Weiss, A. (1994) *Best-Laid Plans: Turning strategy into action throughout your organization*, Las Brisas Resource Press, Shakopee, MN, USA

Weiss, A (2002) *Value-based fees: How to charge and get what you're worth*, Jossey-Bass/Pfeiffer, San Francisco, CA

Let's make a movie 05

Situational inter-organizational relationships

While sustaining long-term strategic relationships is critical for success, an ever more common response to the rapidly changing business environments of today is the formation of short-term alliances designed to address specific tactical goals, projects or initiatives. In many instances these arrangements bring together people from different disciplines who may come from different cultures and ethnic backgrounds. Add in long distances and different time zones and the complexities and challenges of sustaining successful working relationships increase even more. In some cases, these arrangements are one off, in others they may come together several times over an extended period as needed, with some, or all, of the same participants. In all cases it is crucial to manage these arrangements effectively to leverage the strength of this diversity to the benefit of all. Short-term situational working arrangements that are set up between organizations to achieve specific well-defined goals and business outcomes, within well-defined timeframes are an increasingly common phenomenon in modern business. It is fundamentally important to draw clear distinctions between these types of relationships and the longer-term working relationships discussed in Chapter 4. This is because the skills, tools, mindset and temperament required from the participants in short-term situational inter-organizational relationships are quite different from those required for longer-term working arrangements. This has very important implications for all businesses that wish to leverage the dynamism, creativity and innovative outcomes that can be achieved through these types of working arrangements.

One of the pioneering industries in adopting this modus operandi has been the film industry. The process of making a modern movie involves several sequential steps that typically take place over several months to a couple of years and involves a sequence that may involve some, or all, of the following activities:

- story development
- screenwriting
- casting
- shooting
- sound recording
- editing
- screening
- distribution.

Additionally, many different professionals and specialists are involved in this movie-making process, including:

- screenwriters;
- illustrators and artists;
- producers;
- directors;
- financial and insurance specialists;
- sound engineers;
- photographers and camera operators;
- production managers;
- set and costume designers;
- make-up artists and hair stylists;
- production managers; and
- actors and stunt artists.

The making of a movie corresponds to the ideal scenario described that best suits the type of time-bounded working arrangements that we have been discussing. That is, they are relatively short term, a few months to a couple of years, they have a specific well-defined outcome, in this case the production and distribution of a movie, and they involve the participation and collaboration of multiple independent entities for the creation of that desired common outcome. In many cases these projects and multidisciplinary teams are international in nature, work to tight deadlines and within strict financial parameters. Indeed, in many ways they are analogous to many of the short-term working arrangements that are formed and reformed among supply chain partners for specific well-defined projects.

Multidisciplinary teams

For example, in our consultancy business we have worked on several projects for manufacturing clients to help them design and implement new warehousing capacity to support their manufacturing operations. In many cases, while the facilities have been designed to suit the operational requirements of the manufacturers' specific production plants, it will require no capital expenditure on their part. This is being achieved through the bringing together of a multi- disciplinary consortium for this specific purpose that is quite reminiscent of the cast of specialists required to produce a movie as discussed previously. We, as logistics and supply chain specialists, work closely with the manufacturer, our direct client, to define precisely what the operational requirement is and other key parameters are such as the size of the facility and the activities that will be performed within the facility. These activities typically involve receiving materials from suppliers, quality checks, pallet exchange, storage, kitting, issuing material to production, receiving finished goods from production, and shipping as well as the types and classes of materials to be held and handled there such as raw materials, packaging, work in progress and finished goods together with any special hazardous requirements, specifications for temperature and humidity control, chemical storage and other ancillary requirements. We also define the shape, orientation, layout, capacity and performance metrics for the operating facility. This work is done with the active participation of the client's warehouse and manufacturing operations specialists, as well as their facilities managers, environmental health and safety (EHS) managers, quality assurance managers, materials managers, supply chain managers and other relevant stakeholders within the client organization. Thereafter, the client's professional real estate advisors and consultants are engaged to identify suitable, available locations for the facilities close to the production plants that fulfil the operational requirements and parameters that we have defined for the client. Next, qualified investors/developers and service providers are invited to provide proposals to build, operate and lease back the working warehouse facility to the manufacturing client. These investors bring together multidisciplinary teams comprising financiers such as banks and other institutional investors, structural and civil engineers, heating and ventilation engineering specialists, electrical engineers, planning specialists, quantity surveyors, fire protection specialists, legal teams and others. In some instances, the lead investors and developers are also logistics service providers and therefore they also bring in their logistics operating specialists for the design of work processes and the procurement of the storage and materials handling equipment, both conventional and automated that may be required to operate the facility.

These projects typically have a duration of about two years from initial conception to the delivery of the completed operating facility and the different participants and specialists have different roles and responsibilities at different phases throughout the project. Some of the participants, such as ourselves, have a central role from beginning to end as the representative of the client interest throughout the project. The outcome, a facility designed to specification that enables the client's business to grow sustainably in the future based on a long-term lease contract without large capital expenditure together with a long-term guaranteed income and return for the investor that provides a win-win outcome for both parties.

These short-term, inter-disciplinary, inter-organizational and often international working arrangements are becoming ever more common across a range of activities such as collaborative product development between suppliers and OEMs (Original Equipment Manufacturers), particularly in the automotive and aerospace sectors, in consumer product marketing launches and in the provision of emergency aid in response to natural and man-made disasters and humanitarian crises. This type of adhocracy and project-based work has been increasing in scope and frequency in recent decades powered by the advances in information and communications technology (ICT) since around 1990. This has made it possible for geographically dispersed teams to exchange ideas and work in synchronicity on common tasks without the need to be physically present in a face-to-face context. As communications technology continues to advance with big improvements in telepresence applications, in which participants in meetings have the impression of being in a face-to-face meeting through providing the users senses with a range of stimuli to create this effect, the prevalence of these types of working arrangements will tend to increase over time. At the high end, there are telepresence video conferencing applications, such as Cisco TelePresence and Polycom RealPresence, which provide a much higher quality of video and sound than traditional video conferencing applications. While these applications are still quite expensive and difficult to set up, as the technology advances and the costs decrease the benefits of quick response, travel avoidance and productivity increase will become more widely available to businesses and other organizations.

New business models

These capabilities are giving rise to new business models that are built around these technologies enabling dispersed groups of people to carry out work efficiently and cost effectively and to provide services in a seamless manner that would have been very difficult and expensive to do, if not impossible, just 20 or 30 years ago when in all practicality the people would have had to be congregated in the same building to carry out the work effectively. For example, in our own consultancy work, we are now able to access and work effectively with technical specialists all around the world who provide a range of inputs that allows us to work faster, more economically and to bring a wider range of services and capabilities to market than was the case previously. For example, on a recent consultancy project for a multinational manufacturer in the life sciences sector with a production plant in Ireland, we produced a warehouse capacity modelling application to enable 'what-if' future scenarios to be run to predict the impact of various future courses of action or eventualities on future capacity requirements. To do this required various elements of work including data analysis, CAD drawing, mathematical model building as well as project management and ongoing interfacing with the client team. In this project, which we led from our base in Dublin, Ireland we worked with independent associates with specialist skills located in several different countries. Some of the data analysis was done by us in Dublin, Ireland and other elements were carried out by an associate based in El Paso, Texas, USA, the CAD drawing was done by another associate based in Katowice in Poland and the model building was carried out by yet another associate in Zagreb, Croatia with all the proofing, quality control and client interfacing planned, controlled and executed from Dublin, Ireland. Each of these associates have their own independent practices and do other work with other clients in their own localities directly as well as with other associates and yet this is a team that comes together again and again in different combinations, sometimes just two, other times three and yet other times all four depending on the specific requirements of the project.

The team has built a relationship and a way of working that is reignited each time that it comes together. Sometimes the projects work in the opposite direction, with one of the overseas associates leading a project for a client in their region with us carrying out certain elements of the work here in Ireland. This is all made possible through leveraging applications such as cloud-based shared folders and files, video conferencing, email and instant messaging over relatively cheap broadband connections. This is a revolution in service provision that enables us to do in a fraction of the time and cost what would have been hugely expensive and complicated, if at all possible, a little over 10 years ago while at the same time providing access to international markets, otherwise extremely difficult to penetrate.

The reason for this increased prevalence of short-term project-based working arrangements is that they provide many advantages over traditional approaches that involve trying to deliver these outcomes with fully in-house teams with personnel who have other steady-state operational, commercial or technical roles. The advantages include:

- access to a wide range of skills;
- ability to access these skills and capabilities as needed and no requirement to have a permanent overhead on stand-by;
- access to markets and clients in geographically distant locations;
- specialists can gain continuous experience in different projects with same process and cross-pollination of best practices;
- the people involved develop a mindset, and disposition that equips them well for these types of engagements in a way that people trained to work in steady-state operational roles find difficult to adapt to;
- the speed of delivery of projects and set-ups can be accelerated; and
- the ability to measure performance, cost and return on investment.

It is important to note also that these short-term arrangements with specialist teams are being used increasingly to set up and launch longer-term working arrangements. For instance, the selection and appointment of logistics service providers or the introduction of an operational standards and metrics regime for an operating team to measure its performance. These are initiatives that will have a steady-state long-term duration over several years, but that require very short-term initiatives to formulate, implement and embed of just a few weeks. The reason for this is that it is difficult for the people involved in the day-to-day activities of ongoing operations to handle projects effectively. This is because the skills sets required for project work, due to the different cadence, urgency and task types, are very different from those required to be an effective operational manager. When companies peg projects on to the roles and responsibilities of operational managers, these projects often get bogged down and the initiatives peter out in the cut and thrust of the urgencies of day-to-day operations and the inevitable emergencies that occur.

Skills requirements

The skills and ways of working required of the people who work on these types of short-term ad hoc arrangements with specific and well-defined outcomes are quite different from those required for professionals working in long-term steady-state operations as has been already mentioned. Many of the skills required in both types of working arrangements coincide in their broad categorization; however, the way they are applied, and the level of readjustment and adaptability required is of a different order for those involved primarily on short-term working arrangements.

Communication

In terms of communication skills, people involved in short-term working arrangement need to be able to adjust and adapt their communicating styles rapidly. It is not unusual for people in these circumstances to work on several different projects at any one point in time. Some of these projects may last for several months and others over a year and therefore there is a constant churn of new personalities, new communications types and styles and ever-changing roles and responsibilities. In one project, a person may have a lead role and be the director of the action whereas in another project the same person may play a supporting role to another person in the lead position. This requires real breadth and depth of competence and capability in communications to be truly effective. One element of this is the command of language both in form and content. People with a wide and varied vocabulary who can adapt their style and who are competent at transmitting and absorbing information aurally and visually will be best suited to these types of roles. The ability to develop and maintain rapport with other individuals from different organizational and cultural backgrounds is also a very favourable attribute for people who aspire to be effective in these types of roles. This would tend to cover people who have wide international experience or who have had the opportunity to interact professionally with people from many different countries. While multi-lingualism is not necessarily a requirement for success in these types of roles, proficiency in several of the more important global business languages can broaden the scope of opportunity for people in this area.

Flexibility

Because these working arrangements are formed, dissolved, reformed in different formats and configurations over short periods of time, and notwithstanding the fact that there may be a common underlying structure or format to the arrangements, the specific working requirements, expectations, accountabilities and activities for specific individuals will vary greatly from time to time and from project to project. The implication of this is that those people who can adapt to these changes quickly and seamlessly and still perform at their best will be particularly well suited to this type of working. In each project, new relationships are formed, new rules of engagement are established, formal and informal roles change, and sometimes the ranking and pecking order changes depending on the configuration of the project and how each participant or organization came to be part of the project. For example, in some arrangements that I have been involved in personally, I have had people reporting to me on projects when my organization was the lead player and on the next project I was reporting in to that same person because their organization was the lead player.

Technical ability

The range of tools and applications that is available to facilitate the work of teams is evolving all the time. Currently, there are tools for project management such as Basecamp and Teamwork, tools for sharing folders and files such as Google Drive and One Drive, tools for working on such as Google Docs, tools for communicating using audio and video such as Skype and Zoom, as well as high-end video conference telepresence applications such as Cisco TelePresence. New offerings and improved versions of existing applications are becoming available on an ongoing basis and therefore the ability to use and adapt to these types of tools is highly desirable also. Up until quite recently, many large organizations didn't allow the use of many of these applications due principally to security and confidentiality concerns whereas now, more and more organizations large and small are embracing and becoming ever more comfortable with the use of these tools as they come to realize the business benefits that can be achieved in terms of speed, productivity, efficiency and environmental sustainability.

Ability to work fast and slow

One of the most notable characteristics of work on these types of short-term working arrangements is the absence of what might be a fundamental element of steady-state operations and that is the absence of routine or a clearly defined and structured working day. On a given project there may be periods when activity is intense and hectic and there are deadlines to be met while at other times the pace of work decreases as other elements are active. Furthermore, as people can very well be working on several unrelated projects simultaneously, they may find themselves in the situation where one or other project is in a phase of high activity for them while others are in a phase of low activity. The ability to be able to shift between work modes and cadences in short time without losing focus and becoming disoriented and disorganized is also a feature of the people who are best adapted to these roles.

Need for association and affiliation

Different people have different needs for association and affiliation through their work (Weiss, 2011), that is, the sensation and feeling of belonging to something that is durable and stable over an extended period in association with individuals with whom bonds are strengthened and deepened over time. The types of short-term working arrangements that we are discussing in this section are best suited to people who have lower requirements for this type of association and affiliation through their work and who have a frame of reference for job satisfaction and feedback that is more internally focused. They tend to be people who, while they are comfortable working in teams and collaborating with others, they can also adapt to working alone and generating their own motivation, planning and organization when the need arises.

Technology and applications

Some of the applications that are available and used most commonly for collaborative work on short-term project-based work include some of the following:

Basecamp

Basecamp is a web-based project management application that allows geographically dispersed teams to work in concert using shared to-do lists, to assign tasks to each other and to converse by text and exchange documents and files in a forum-like environment and to provide work progress updates that are visible to all participants. There are various subscription levels available depending on the requirements and complexity of the organization and the projects that are being worked on.

Google Docs

Google Docs, together with Google Sheets and Google Slides, is a word processor, a spreadsheet and a presentation program available for free from Google as a web-based software office suite. There are other add-on applications available and the distinguishing feature is that the suite allows geographically dispersed users to work collaboratively on single documents and to edit and track changes in these documents in real time.

Google Drive

Google Drive is a file storage and synchronization service that allows users to store files locally and to synchronize those files across devices and to share those files. It is possible to do this with files of all types. For example, an architect may be working on a CAD drawing of a high-level design for a building. She saves that drawing to the shared file on her own laptop and shares with a technician in a different location with instructions to include further details on the drawing. The technician adds the detail and saves to the file on his machine. The updated file then synchronizes across the devices using the internet and the architect can review the updated details on the drawing. Google Drive offers users free storage and provides options to increase the storage capacity through paid plans.

Skype

Skype is a telecommunications app that provides internet voice telephony and video calls, including conference video calls between computers as well as between mobile devices such as tablets and smartphones. Skype also allows for instant messaging and file transfers including text, image and video files. Skype was acquired by Microsoft in 2011, and in 2015 Microsoft released Skype for Business, which combines features of Microsoft's previous offering Lync with those of the original consumer software Skype. Skype for Business is enterprise software and since its availability many large organizations that were previously reluctant to use the consumer software offering from Skype have deployed Skype for Business as their preferred telephony and video chat application.

Zoom

Zoom is a communications application that provides video conferencing, online meetings and mobile collaboration and was founded by engineers from Cisco and WebEx. Zoom combines HD video conferencing, online business meetings, webinars and mobile capabilities. One of the interesting features is that only one user needs to download Zoom while all the other users can simply click on the meeting link and access the meeting from their device, whether a phone, tablet or computer. Both screen sharing as well as video conferencing are possible simultaneously to facilitate active working meetings.

WhatsApp

WhatsApp is an instant messaging service for smartphones that allows for the creation of groups and the exchange of files including images, audio and video files. WhatsApp also provides Voice over IP (VoIP) service and uses standard cell phone numbers. As such it is a quick and easy way to communicate with contacts around the world in an efficient and economical manner.

Cisco telepresence

Cisco telepresence is designed to link two or more rooms that are separated geographically in such a way as to give the impression to people that they are all present in one single room. The distinction between telepresence and video conferencing provided by applications such as Skype and Zoom is the quality, simplicity and reliability that can be achieved and they are designed specifically for the remote participants to feel as if they were present in the same room in what is termed an 'immersive collaborative experience' and to achieve this they utilize a range of special equipment including flat screen displays, special tables, microphones, loudspeakers, cameras and lighting.

This is just a small sample of the tools and applications that are available and that are driving the increased adoption of dynamic, multidisciplinary multilocation working teams that are being an ever more common feature of modern business and of the types of working relationships in international supply chains.

Examples of short-term collaborative working arrangements

We are going to explore a number of case studies of real-life projects in which we have had first-hand experience and where these types of arrangements were put in place to deliver specific well-defined outcomes and we are going to discuss the goal of the project, the activities that were carried out and the various participants that contributed to the project as well as the challenges that were encountered and the final outcome of the project.

Warehouse design and logistics service provider selection and for manufacturer in the consumer food industry

In this project, the objective of the manufacturer was to ensure the future provision of capacity for the storage of finished product in an environment where volumes were growing rapidly and the possibilities of expanding the warehousing facilities at the plant were limited. To determine the future requirements and potential options, the management formed a team composed of internal and external specialists whose task was to work together to determine what the future warehousing and distribution requirements would be over five- and 10-year time horizons under several future growth scenarios. The team was made up of an internal lead in the person of the operations director who assembled a working group of internal and external specialists. Internally, the main participants were the commercial manager to provide insight into future volume requirements, production and operations managers to provide input on the material flow and process requirements for receipt, storage, picking and shipping of the product and internal information technology and business systems specialists who would be required to extract relevant data from the enterprise system to enable other specialists to carry out data analysis and capacity projections. In terms of external specialists, the company engaged the services of a business consultancy specialized in the distribution systems optimization, which in turn associated with a second business consultancy specialized in the optimization of warehouse layouts, work processes and inventory deployment and slotting. A firm of structural engineers and architects were also engaged to work in collaboration with the business consultants to explore the practical options for expansion of the on-site facilities to cater for future capacity requirements.

In the first phase of the work the business consultants specified the data requirements to the internal IT specialists who extracted the data in accordance with the specification. The external consultants then analysed the data and developed a future projection of the warehouse size, capacity, layout, storage equipment and manning levels required, together with the requirements for distribution in terms of routes, frequencies and destinations. Together with the architects and engineers, several on-site options were developed and reviewed with the project owner. What became apparent from this work was that the internal capital expenditure required, combined with the physical limitations of the existing site, made the option difficult to justify in terms of return on investment and risk. This conclusion led to the second phase of the project, in which the business consultants developed alternative options by developing a detailed specification for the operation of the warehousing and distribution functions to be carried on externally from the business and engaging with several qualified logistics service providers. This phase of the project involved wider engagement with several prospective partners to ensure that they understood the requirements and could make realistic proposals to the client. Evaluation of these proposals led to the selection of a preferred provider and the negotiation of a contract of engagement.

This was then followed by the implementation phase involving the transfer of inventory, alignment of IT systems and set up of communications protocols between the teams on the client side and on the service provider side to ensure smooth transition to the steady-state operating regime. Through this solution, the client was able to access a cost-effective and flexible solution, without a large capital expenditure and with guaranteed levels of performance and costs over an extended period.

The project from beginning to end was approximately 12 months and during that period different specialists contributed to the tasks and activities in different ways. Some were more active in certain phases and less active in others. Some carried out different activities or exited the project altogether as the requirements changed and evolved. This was a dynamic and flexible process that delivered the tangible business result of a sustainable distribution logistics solution for the business after having analysed all feasible options for both internal and external solutions. One of the main challenges experienced by the team during the work was associated with the project management and coordination role. This is a role that is often overlooked in these projects and in the absence of its formal and explicit definition and specification, the various participants in the project are sometimes unsure of their role, responsibilities, accountabilities and communications channels. The coordinating role will often end up falling by default on the project owner which is rarely the most effective outcome. In the next case we will see an example of a project where this important coordinating role was covered in a very explicit manner and where the number and geographical dispersion of the participants in the project was far greater than in the case just discussed.

Installation of an automated storage retrieval system for printed media

In this project the requirement was to specify, select and install an automated storage and retrieval solution for printed media in a new-build facility. This element of the project was a specialist requirement within a wider and somewhat more conventional requirement for the design, construction and commissioning of a multi-use building. These automated storage and retrieval solutions are essentially composed of three main components – a shelving or racking structure onto which boxes and bins that contain the inventory are placed for storage, a storage and retrieval machine or crane that runs in the aisle space between the rows of shelving and which can put away and retrieve storage bins from the multiple locations within the shelving as required and a software solution that controls and coordinates the movements of the crane in response to demands and orders that come through a software interface to the business enterprise system that processes the orders for receipt and put away from the system users.

In this case, a team was put together involving key stakeholders from within the client organization including both systems end users and IT specialists together with a host of external specialists including a consulting engineering and project management firm, a firm of architects and structural engineers, a construction company and a materials handling systems specialist consultancy responsible for the specification of the automated storage and retrieval solution and for guiding and advising the client on the selection of the preferred solution vendor and integrator.

Worldwide, the number of systems integration companies capable of delivering an automated storage and retrieval system of this nature is quite limited. Additionally, all of them are headquartered in countries far from the installation location. Consequently, the selection process required interaction with several bidders located in different countries around the world. In some instances, project meetings took place using video conferencing facilities with participants contributing simultaneously from locations in Ireland, the US, the UK and Spain. The presence of an explicit coordinating function in the project management role proved to be essential for the efficiency and effectiveness of the project, particularly in the implementation phase, when the level of detail and the frequency of communication for decision-making was very intense and needed to be very precise. Some of the major challenges that arose and that involved extra effort was the careful communication required to align expectations, interpretations and specific technical requirements and standards across international borders between Europe and North America. For instance, the production of the training and maintenance manuals in the US meant that references to dimensions in feet and inches and references to US engineering, safety and environmental standards had to be changed to metric measures and to the equivalent European standards.

Upgrade to a specialist internal logistics operations and information systems across multiple sites

This is a project that required the coordination of a multidisciplinary team responsible for a specialist internal logistics operation for special materials separate from the wider logistics operations of several production plants located in Europe, North America and South America. The objective of the project was to unify the operating regime across the sites, while setting inventory levels and mixes in ways to maximize the robustness of the international inventory strategy from a business continuity planning point of view and to unify the locations through the integration of one single information system solution for the tracking of inventory and the management of the inventory in the various locations in real time.

The team was composed of managers and operators from the larger of the sites situated in Europe, who, together with an external warehouse operations specialist, were responsible for defining the optimum operating regime and ways of working in the facilities. This was then translated into a User Requirement Specification (URS), for the information management system functionality that would be required to support the operating requirements of the business in Europe that were to be mirrored in the North American and South American operations. The administrative team, whose input was also required as part of the functionality specification for the information system was in North America. The project owner who was based in the European operation was responsible for coordinating the overall project and reporting progress to the project sponsor based in the US. One significant aspect of the project was that the European operation created and implemented a new way of working for the storage and retrieval of materials in the storage systems. This new process helped to improve space utilization, stock rotation and operator productivity. Consequently, this improvement needed to be deployed in the North American and South American operations. Furthermore, an information systems solution needed to be selected from a range of vendor offerings and deployed across the three locations while being controlled from the administrative hub in North America.

Some of the challenges encountered on this project were again related to communication and coordination among the teams from the different countries. This was partly driven by the different time zones and working times of the people in the different locations and partly to do with the interpretation and understanding of the challenges presented by working with people across borders with different cultures, working in some cases through a language, English, that was not their first language. On the other hand, the fact that most of the participants in the project were employees of one large international organization meant that many difficulties that might otherwise be encountered within an ad hoc multinational project like this were overcome through the common organizational culture, shared jargon, expectations and accountabilities. This project heavily leveraged communications technology such as video conferencing to reduce the requirements for intercontinental travel, to accelerate decision-making and to increase overall productivity.

Summary

In this chapter we have described the short-term, interdisciplinary working arrangements that are becoming an ever more common feature of supply chain working arrangements as being analogous to the production teams that have been the bedrock of movie making for many years. The distinction being that today, innovations in information and communications technology have empowered organizations to leverage the capabilities of internal and external specialists often geographically dispersed, but who can now work together almost as if they were present in the same physical location. We have also seen that in the provision of certain professional services, these innovations and changes in ways of working are giving rise to new business models of associates and companies that come together, disperse and reform in different combinations to provide tailored, as needed services to deliver well-defined business outcomes with tangible business benefits and easily identifiable return on investment.

We have also explained how these types of working relationship require the development of the key skills of communication, flexibility and cultural awareness to be applied in new and dynamic ways that are substantially different to what is required from professionals who are accustomed to working in day-to-day operations with structured work cycles and routines. We have reviewed a small selection of the myriad tools and applications that are now being provided and improved by developers and technology companies that are enabling more and more companies to take advantage of these forms of working and to partake in the benefits of speed, efficiency and sustainability that result. Finally, we described a small selection of real-life projects where these types of working arrangements, tools and technologies have been applied, ranging from the delivery of specific infrastructure, to operational change and performance improvement and to the setting up of new inter-organizational working arrangements such as the outsourcing of distribution warehousing and transport. While the applications are very different, they have all benefited from the advantages that these short-term working relationships can deliver by leveraging modern technology and skills sets.

Reference

Weiss, A (2011) *The Consulting Bible: Everything you need to know to create and expand a seven-figure consulting practice*, John Wiley & Sons, Hoboken, NJ

Why bother?

The whole is greater than the sum of the parts

Why are supply-chain interfaces so important to the success and sustainability of supply chain relationships? If the supply chain is thought of as a complex adaptive system, then it will be seen to exhibit emergent properties (OU, 2016) such as speed, flexibility and cost-effectiveness that will translate to business benefits for the supply chain as a whole that it would not have been possible for the components of the system to achieve in isolation. In effect, the whole is greater than the sum of the parts. However, for a supply chain to be a truly effective system, the links and connections at the interfaces between the components need to be effective. To apply the tools and techniques of supply chain management to full effect it is essential to understand that the roots of supply chain management go back to the intellectual framework of systems thinking and its fundamental concepts of components, boundaries, connections, purpose, emergence and sub-optimization (OU, 2016). Let's first take a look at the key concepts of systems thinking and why it is so important to unlock the full potential of the supply chain.

Systems thinking

Every business forms part of a supply chain or more accurately it forms part of multiple supply chains or productive networks, acting as both supplier to its customers and customer to its suppliers. However, while every company is part of the supply chain and carries on a range of supply chain functions including logistics, production, sales, marketing and after-sales service, not every company is doing supply chain management. How can this be, you may ask. We are carrying out supply chain activities and we are managing our business, hence we are doing supply chain management, right? No, wrong! So, what is the distinction? The key distinction is that supply chain management requires us to really understand and apply the key concepts of systems thinking (OU, 2016) and to adopt a systems approach to organizing, managing and measuring the activities of the business. Systems thinking is a way of considering sets of interrelated components and activities as a complex adaptive system with a defined goal or purpose, with clear boundaries between those components that belong to the system and those components that do not. Adopting a systems approach involves looking at the behaviour of this whole system or supply chain, rather than the traditional reductionist approach (OU, 2016) that breaks the system down into its component parts and analyses the behaviour of each component individually. This alternative 'systems' perspective will very often give rise to some rather surprising and counterintuitive insights. We will come back to what it means to view a supply chain from this perspective later, but for now let's take a more accessible example to illustrate what I mean.

An everyday complex system

One of the most significant characteristics of this holistic, systems approach to analysis is that it allows us to detect the emergent properties of the system. These are properties that simply cannot be perceived at the component level of analysis. This is, in effect, the essence of the statement that 'the whole is greater than the sum of the parts' and can be difficult to grasp fully at first. By way of an example, think about a very common complex system that most people are familiar with such as an airplane. This system is made up of thousands of components including aluminium panels, rivets, turbine blades, printed circuits, software code and so on. No amount of analysis at the component level, of the dimensions, the shapes, or the constituent materials of these components would allow you to detect, observe or measure the emergent property of this system that is flight. The right combination of these components will produce this emergent property when assembled into an airplane. To consider the various aspects of flight you must analyse the assembled system, the whole airplane, as one integrated system. In effect, an airplane is a complex system composed of a multitude of interconnected components with a purpose – to transport people and freight, and a clear boundary, the landing gear is in the system and the runway is outside, and flight is one of its emergent properties. One important point to note also with regard to the boundaries of the system, is that depending who is interested in the system and what their goals are, the boundary of the system may change. For example, if I am an aeronautical engineer interested in optimizing the flight characteristics of an aircraft, I may be interested in the system that is limited to the physical aircraft itself. If I am a business analyst with an airline carrier, I might be interested in analysing the performance of a wider system including the aircraft, but also the crew, the passengers and the airport, for the purpose of optimizing the use of the aircraft assets for revenue generation.

Now consider a typical supply chain, let's say in the coffee industry. The components of this system include the producers and harvesters of the coffee beans in several developing economies around the world; Brazil, Vietnam, Colombia and Peru are among the major producers. Then there are the coffee consolidators, often cooperatives, that consolidate the coffee production of multiple small producers and supply the large coffee processors, roasters and blenders. Thereafter, come the coffee importers, the wholesalers and the retailers including general grocery and supermarket retailers as well as specialized coffee shops, service stations and restaurateurs. To this we could add several other players such as transport, warehousing and distribution services providers, traders and brokers. This is a complex, multi-tier supply chain with many interacting and interconnected components with a purpose – the classic definition of a system. Depending on my position in this supply chain, the system of interest, its inputs, outputs, performance and the boundary that I draw around it will vary. For example, if I am one of the global big-brand coffee-shop retailers I will perhaps be interested in a system that includes the processors and the importers/wholesalers, as well as the international transport, warehousing and distribution logistics service providers, my retail outlets and customers to understand how best I can guarantee the supply and quality of the coffee that I need in all my coffee shops around the world, while at the same time balancing the working capital tied up in inventory and my controlling total operating costs. If I am a cooperative coffee consolidator in, say, Colombia, my system of interest might be the one that encompasses the farmers and harvesters, the coffee processors in Colombia and the local transport service providers. The aspects of the performance of this supply chain that I am interested in may be production input costs and the sustainability of the price that can be paid to the producers to ensure their ability to maintain production and a reasonably consistent level of income over time.

One of the most powerful concepts within systems thinking is the concept of sub-optimization. This concept provides the fundamental insight that you cannot optimize the performance of the overall system by optimizing the performance of each individual component individually. Attempting to do this is in fact dysfunctional and will lead to the sub-optimization of the performance of the overall system. To optimize the overall system performance, you will need to change the level of analysis from the individual component to the whole system so that you will be able to clearly see and understand the key variables, inputs and outputs, that affect and denote the performance of the overall system. You cannot do this at the component level. In practice, this may translate into consciously accepting the sup-optimal performance of some components of the system as a trade-off in order to optimize the overall system performance.

This can be a tricky concept to understand intellectually and an even trickier one to apply in practice, yet it is one of the most powerful insights provided by the systems approach to managing complex systems such as supply chains. By way of example, I recently visited the distribution centre of a very large food retail chain. The distribution centre provides daily supply and replenishment of grocery products to approximately 50 supermarket outlets situated within a radius of about 60 km. Orders are received from the supermarket managers and warehouse operatives in the central distribution warehouse using handheld devices that direct them to where to find the required products, pick the ordered products by the case in the quantity required. In the distribution centre, the products are stored on pallets in high-bay pallet racking systems. On the accessible ground levels of these racking systems, pallets of product are located in 'pick face' locations that are fixed by product from where the pickers pick the products by the case onto the order pallets and cages that they move around the warehouse from pick location to pick location with the aid of powered pallet trucks. This is a labour- and asset-intensive activity, which in a large distribution centre requires many people travelling long distances to carry out this physical work. This is a situation where an optimization of the location of the product on the pick faces within the warehouse as a function of the frequency of requirement and volume of throughput can yield very high productivity increases.

However, I noticed as I observed the pickers doing their work that, while there had been a certain optimization of pick face layout by categories, they had not pursued this optimization to its full potential at the individual SKU (Stock Keeping Unit) level. When I enquired why this was the case, the operations manager explained that in their strategy they focus on optimization of the overall system output at the retail store – maximize retail space, minimal staffing, quick replenishment with minimum disruption at store level and maximized sale per square metre. As a consequence, they came to the conscious conclusion that in order to achieve these systemic outcomes at the retail customer interface for the greater good of the overall business, they needed to accept a certain 'inefficiency' or sub-optimization of order picking at the distribution centre. They did this consciously in full awareness of a greater gain elsewhere for the overall business system. They had understood the concept of sub-optimization and they had translated it successfully into practice in the real world. This was, in effect, conscious and aware supply chain management in practice.

What you choose to optimize at the aggregate system level will be dependent on the strategy that you are pursuing and the goals that you are trying to achieve. For example, if the business has a strategy of differentiation you will pursue objectives related to quality, service and brand prestige, whereas if your business strategy is one of cost leadership you will likely be pursuing goals related to cost management, efficiency and resource optimization. In both cases, you can apply a systemic supply chain management approach to optimizing overall system performance, yet the goals you will seek to achieve, and what outputs you will choose to optimize at the system level, and as a consequence what sub-optimization choices you make at the component level, will be very different. It is the conscious and informed application of systems thinking to the design, implementation and management of supply chains that is the key distinction between simply forming part of a supply chain, as all businesses do, and truly applying supply chain management (SCM) in practice as a competitive tool, which most businesses do not. In effect, supply chain management is by definition a systems approach to the conception, design and management of supply chains. Put bluntly, if you are not applying systems thinking and a systems approach to understanding and improving your supply chain then you are not doing supply chain management.

Specialization and the focus on core competences

In the 1910s and 1920s, The Ford Motor Company (FMC, 2018) leveraged the technologies and processes of mass production to revolutionize the industrial production of standardized products, in this case motors in the form of the famous Ford Model T, in a way that that provided quality, reliability and affordability. The Ford Motor Company of that time was characterized by the way in which it was vertically integrated as a business, that is, that large parts of the company's supply chain were not just controlled, but were actually owned, by the company. Indeed, in the 1920s the Ford River Rouge Complex was manufacturing most of the steel used in the production of Ford's automobiles rather than the firm buying the steel from external suppliers. Vertical integration – both backwards integration to the ownership of the primary production and sourcing of raw material inputs and forward integration to the ownership of wholesale and retail distribution channels – was a business strategy that enabled large corporations to capture the lion's share of the value of the products and to control costs, quality and supply. This was a strategy particularly suited to situations and circumstances where supply and distribution networks did not previously exist, were immature or simply did not have the capacity or capability required to manage the effective and efficient flows of product, information and finance through the supply chain. Indeed, in the early and middle decades of the 20th century, it was not uncommon for many large corporations to own primary production, secondary production, transport, distribution and retail, as well as providing, in-house, all the ancillary services from facility management to accounting, to cleaning and even canteen catering for employees.

The advantages of vertical integration for a corporation are easy to see. Firstly, it provides the corporation with the possibility to monopolize its market and to lower transaction costs in the supply chain. It provides the business with a degree of independence from the uncertainties associated with relying on third parties and enables a greater degree of control over the planning of supply and demand. However, some of the vulnerabilities of the highly vertically integrated enterprise include inflexibility and an inability to change direction quickly, or adapt to new circumstances as a result of the asset trap of the ownership and control of production facilities and technologies, transport assets, and real estate.

From the 1970s onwards, however, global economic volatility began to increase due to geopolitical, technological and demographic trends, and companies in the more developed countries began to expand their businesses in a process of economic globalization as a response to both home-market saturation and competitive pressures from ever more demanding and empowered consumers. This gave rise to increased complexity in the international supply chains of these businesses coupled with a relentless pressure to adapt and innovate in response to changing circumstances on a permanent basis. This new reality exposed the vulnerabilities and weaknesses of the highly vertically integrated enterprise and many companies began to divest themselves of the assets and activities that they considered non-essential to their ability to deliver value to their customers. Indeed, in 1990 CK Prahalad and Gary Hamel articulated this process when they published an article in the *Harvard Business Review* called 'the core competences of the corporation' (Pralahad and Hamel, 1990). Prahalad and Hamel identified the core competences of a business as those skills and resources that are critical to the company in delivering value to the customer and that are difficult for competitors to imitate. In effect, they stated that the development of core competencies would trump vertical integration in the new globally competitive economic environment. As a result of this shift in perspective, new business strategies were adopted that focused ever more narrowly on committing resources to developing core competencies such as certain technologies, processes or capabilities and contracting or buying in other services and inputs that supported and enabled the core activities. This gave rise to a wave of downsizing and outsourcing on the part of many large, formerly highly vertically integrated enterprises together with the emergence of a plethora of new niche suppliers and service providers who developed core competences in many of the activities that the larger corporations were relinquishing.

This new arrangement brought with it the advantage of focus, flexibility and agility and released many enterprises from the asset trap of vertical integration, allowing them to be more nimble and adaptive to changing circumstances. What this change also brought with it was a marked increase in the level of complexity involved in dealing with many more external suppliers of products, materials and services that were essential to the ability of the organization to conduct its business and satisfy the needs of its customers. The types of relationships and interactions required to manage a business based on myriad strategic long- and short-term relationships with a plethora of third-party entities was very different from what had come before. The skills needed and the quality of the relationships and interactions that would bring success were also very different and of a higher order than had previously been the case. While in theory the promise of the focus on core competences together with the leveraging of the expertise and experience of outside suppliers and service providers who were experts in their own fields was that the overall performance of the business would be enhanced, this could only be achieved in practice if new ways of managing the complexity, leveraging the strength of all the partners and measuring the performance of the supply chain as a holistic system were developed and perfected.

Thus emerged through practice, trial and error, the concepts, techniques and tools of the systemic discipline that would eventually be baptized by Keith Oliver, a consultant with Booz Allen Hamilton, as 'supply chain management' (Heckman, Shorten and Engel, 2003) in a 1982 interview with the *Financial Times*. Keith Oliver himself described supply chain management (SCM) as the management of a chain of supply as if it were a single entity – this was indeed a silo-busting, systems approach to understanding and managing the interconnected production networks that were emerging as firms transformed themselves to cope with an ever more diverse and globalized competitive environment. Since that time, the field has broadened and deepened and many organizations have taken the concepts and practices and applied them to gain significant dramatic competitive advantage over their competitors. In the process, many have created new products and services that deliver consistently high levels of quality at prices that would have been unthinkable in the more constrained economic paradigms of the 1950s, 60s and 70s.

Think of the trajectory of organizations such as Apple, Walmart, Tesco, Ryanair, Tata and many others since the time in the 1980s when the concepts and ideas of supply chain management were coalescing into a coherent framework for managing modern business operations internationally. Apple was founded in 1976 by three young men, Steve Jobs, Steve Wozniak and Ronald Wayne, to sell the Apple I (Dernbach, 2018), which was essentially an assembled circuit board without a casing, a keyboard or a monitor. Today Apple is a $215 billion business with 116,000 employees and emblematic products such at the iPhone, the Mac and Apple TV. In 1984, Ryanair commenced operations with one 15-seater aircraft flying from the small regional airport of Waterford in the south of Ireland to London's Gatwick airport. Today, Ryanair is Europe's largest airline by passenger numbers with 11,000 employees and sales of €6.5 billion (Ryanair, 2018). Tesco and Walmart, although already decades old in the 1980s, were still essentially regional players in their home countries at that time, Tesco in southern England and Walmart in the southern and mid-western states of the United States. Today both companies are global retailing behemoths that have expanded their operations worldwide and diversified their offerings far beyond their grocery origins. Tesco currently has sales of £55 billion and employs over 475,000 people (Statista, 2017a) while Walmart has sales of $485 billion and some 2.3 million employees (Statista, 2018). Tata, also a company with a long history going back to 19th-century Mumbai, India, has transformed itself into a global industrial conglomerate since the 1980s with divisions producing steel, motor cars, energy and chemicals. Today it has 660,000 employees and sales of $103 billion (Statista, 2017b). What all of these companies have in common is that they have put the diverse aspects of supply chain management relevant to their circumstances into practice to dramatic effect. This has enabled them to build and manage global networks that are bound together by relationships and interactions with myriad suppliers and service providers as well as their own diverse operations in dozens of countries all around the world. This success can be emulated by any business by pragmatic implementation of a supply chain management approach to managing supplier and customer relationships in a way that makes the whole greater than the sum of the parts.

Applying supply chain management

The key strategies that you can employ to achieve these supply chain advantages are:

- focus on core competences;
- manage the supplier base effectively; and
- develop inter-organizational process improvement.

Even today, many small- and medium-sized companies are excessively vertically integrated and as a consequence are caught in an asset trap that obfuscates their strategic thinking and leaves them vulnerable to competition from more agile competitors that can appear out of nowhere and who are unencumbered with legacy assets and technologies. These marauders can nimbly swoop and eat the lunch of the incumbents. A good example of this is the demise of the video rental giant Blockbuster. In 2004 Blockbuster was at the zenith of its success, with 9,000 video rental stores and 60,000 employees and yet by 2010 it filed for bankruptcy and by 2013 ceased to be

(Philips and Ferdman, 2013). Among the major contributing factors to the demise of Blockbuster was the emergence of Netflix with an offering that included a flat fee, unlimited rentals, no late fees, and a business model unencumbered with the asset trap of expensive stores in prime retail locations (*Harvard Business Review*, 2018), which Blockbuster could not compete with. The concept of focusing on core competitiveness is very much related to concept of the strategic Driving Force® of the business developed by the New Jersey-based business consultancy Kepner-Tregoe (Kepner-Tregoe, 2018). This approach helps a company to identify what products and services the organization will offer and what markets it will serve. Unless, your company is a portfolio business that will enter pretty much any sector in order to make money, the driving force of your business is unlikely to be return/profit. The other possible driving forces are:

- products offered;
- production capability;
- market needs;
- natural resources;
- method of sale;
- method of distribution;
- size/growth; and
- technology.

For example, I recently worked with the management team of an SME whose driving force was market needs but that was operating as if its driving force was production capability. They had particular knowledge and expertise developed over many years that enabled them to determine the product needs and requirements of their market and client base and in identifying and sourcing those products on a worldwide basis. However, they were encumbered with a distribution warehouse facility and operation that had become an obstacle to the further expansion of their product portfolio and sales growth by virtue of the limitations in capacity of the facility, the site it occupied, the skills base of the workforce, and the legacy technology and equipment in the facility. Additionally, the owners of the company were not willing to sanction the capital investments that would have been required to develop a new distribution facility to accommodate future business growth, with up-to-date systems and equipment and an expanded and highly trained workforce. As a result of this process, they came to the conclusion that the best course of action for the future development of the business that would allow them to fully focus on their core competence while availing of the best in class logistics, warehousing and distribution capability that would be scalable with the growth of their business, was to enter into an outsourced warehousing and distribution contract with a best-in-class logistics service provider. As well as outsourcing logistics functions as illustrated in this example, the shift to focus on core competences has led to the outsourcing of a wide range of non-core business support activities such as such as catering, cleaning, security, human resource management, legal services and information technology among others.

Inter-organizational relationships

In the early days, as firms moved away from vertical integration to focus more and more on core competences they began to interact frequently with a greater number of suppliers. Initially, the relationships with many suppliers were adversarial and transaction based with a narrow focus on price and cost which resulted in frequent changes of supply source as a narrow function of this criterion. In years past, working with companies in the medical devices sector that purchase many commoditized parts and components, we have found that procurement departments acting on the transactional-lowest-price model caused a proliferation of SKU item codes, packaging formats, and variable quality of supplier components that led to an explosion of complexity in the management of transport, warehousing and material flows as well as non-value-added increases in inventory and working capital tied up in that inventory. Working capital that could have been put to better use elsewhere in the business. As the process of vertical disintegration unfolded over time, those leading-edge companies that grasped first the systemic nature of supply chain management, and the importance of quality business relationships in that paradigm, began to develop more sophisticated mutually beneficial relationships with their supplier bases. They realized that there are two sides to managing the suppler base more effectively – one is the reduction in the overall number of suppliers to single or dual supply for most requirements and the second is a deepening of the supplier relationships with those suppliers that have a critical strategic role to play in the competitiveness and continuity of the business. Many companies, such as Boeing, Merck, Intel, Ford and many more through the 1990s and 2000s drastically reduced their supplier bases.

One early example of the development of supplier–customer relationships designed to deliver benefits to both parties by breaking down inter-organizational barriers, sharing information, developing joint projects and initiatives was the supply chain coordination initiatives between Walmart and one of its major suppliers, Procter & Gamble (Waller, 2013). Prior to this collaboration, the relationship between the two companies had been adversarial, transactional and fragmented among their many divisions and regions. Interactions were limited to day-to-day, buy–sell transactions with no sharing of information, and no visibility of longer-term requirements, planning or coordination. Through the sharing of information, leveraging technologies such as electronic data interchange (EDI) using standardized formats, and working together on the planning and forecasting of replenishment requirements, they were able to achieve benefits that delivered value to both of their businesses as well as to their common customer, the consumer. These benefits included increased inventory turns, decreased inventory levels, increased logistics efficiency in warehousing and transport, and enhanced customer experience.

These kinds of initiatives require a different kind of relationship and trust between the parties and a different way of thinking about cost and benefit. In some circumstances, it may be beneficial for a customer to invest in the development of a supplier to help them to enhance their knowledge, resources, processes and capabilities in a sort of enlightened self-interest. Toyota and Honda have developed these kinds of initiatives to a significant degree and not just with their supplier bases in Japan within a homogenous cultural environment but also with their suppliers in the US, Canada and Mexico for their production requirement in North America. In my own work with a multinational pharmaceutical manufacturer, I worked directly on an initiative of this nature. The manufacturing company, my client, operated a long-standing service contract with a logistics service provider to manage inbound flows of raw materials and packaging as well as outbound flows of finished product through the provision of off-site warehousing facilities. In this initiative, I worked on behalf of the manufacturer to develop improved processes and capabilities within the business of the logistics service provider. In effect, the manufacturer invested in improving the service provider's processes and capabilities in order to ensure that they could handle significant increases in the throughput volume on the manufacturer's business while at the same time holding down unit operating costs and the resulting charges for services provided. The logistics services provider, for their part, were able to leverage their new learning in other parts of their business on service contracts with other non-competing manufacturers.

This initiative required significant changes in the ways of working of both parties that were challenging for the people involved. These changes ranged from modifications to the timing, content and coordination of activities to the provision and sharing of relevant information, as well as the ongoing measurement and review of performance. These changes took a good deal of purposeful design and implementation in stages that was challenging for all involved but that ultimately established a working relationship that was beneficial to all and that delivered real business benefits to both service provider and customer.

Governance and control

One of the greatest challenges to the full realization of the promise of supply chain management's systemic approach to maximizing business value is the asymmetry in size and power that exists between many of the supply chain partners that interface with each other in the myriad relationships that make up the fabric of modern production networks. In effect, some players are just so much bigger and more powerful than others, and therefore the tensions associated with the governance and control of supply chains and the capturing of the value created in these supply chains is a constant feature of supply chain relationships. Indeed, some organizations hold such a dominant position in the value chain that they are in effect the de facto controllers of the supply network's value creation and this puts them in a position to set the rules of the game and appropriate the lion's share of the value created. Think of the position that companies such as Apple, Walmart, Toyota and Tesco occupy in the global production networks that they form part of, and the level of control they exercise over the firms that make up the supplier bases of these networks. These very large supply chain companies, controlling producers in the case of Apple and Toyota and controlling buyers in the case of Tesco and Walmart, hold sway over the key strategic functions of product design, logistics, sales and marketing. It might be feared that such asymmetries may lead to abuse and exploitation of the smaller parties in the relationships that materialize as constant pressures to reduce prices to guarantee repeat business and it is true that this does happen where supplies are very commoditized.

However, where quality, innovation and compliance are at a premium the dynamics of the network relationships, which involve both a diversification of suppliers' customer bases, as well as a mutual vested interest in success, together with the growing importance of corporate social responsibility and the need to maintain stability and learning do tend to mitigate the asymmetry of the relationship. What many of the lead companies came to realize was that although they might take steps to optimize the core processes over which they retained direct control, in the context of the overall system or production network, that was only a very small proportion of the potential for improvement to unlock competitive advantage; the rest lay in the domain of their supply chain partners and suppliers.

The key for the smaller players in these relationships is to avoid being viewed as the simple vendor of a commoditized product or service and to invest continuously and proactively in the supply chain relationships with the larger supply chain partners through strategies and initiatives that include information sharing, joint development initiatives, cross training and crossover personnel deployment to ensure that quality, speed and alignment to specific requirements can be satisfied. These are actions that tend to deepen the bond, to make it more difficult to replace the supplier, and to ensure that the relationship becomes more strategic and valuable to both parties. In their book, *Lean Solutions: How companies and customers can create value and wealth together*, James P Womack and Daniel T Jones describe how they discovered, while visiting companies in Japan in the early 1980s, that the Toyota Motor Company had achieved a level of excellence that they had not seen before in Japan or in the US through a combination of a focus on the optimization of their core processes, management and control of product development and production, and excellent coordination and collaboration with their suppliers and customers. In effect, they had applied supply chain management principles successfully in such a way that the whole was greater than the sum of the parts of the production network that they had built to produce their motor cars.

Summary

In this chapter we have explored the concept of systems thinking and examined how it is the foundation of the intellectual framework that has evolved and formalized itself since the 1980s as a set of tools and techniques that can help businesses understand and manage the global production networks of which they now form part. This set of tools and techniques has come to be known as supply chain management (SCM), a term coined by Keith Oliver, a consultant with the firm Booz Allen Hamilton consultants in a 1982 interview for the *Financial Times*. In systems thinking, these complex adaptive systems possess specific attributes that define them and that provide insights into their behaviour, and how that behaviour can be shaped and adapted by proactively designing, implementing and measuring the system as a whole. These attributes include:

- **components**, which may be companies, people or assets;
- a **boundary**, which defines what is inside the system and what is outside the system;
- **connections** or links between the components, which indicate how they influence each other and how things such as materials, information and money flow between the components of the system;

- **emergence** or properties that are only observable and measurable at the aggregate level of the whole system and not at the level of the individual components;

- **sub-optimization** or the phenomenon whereby attempted optimization of all components of the system is dysfunctional because it leads to sub-optimization of the performance of the system as a whole; and

- **purpose** or the fact that they system is of interest to us because it exists to achieve some sort of outcome or goal.

We examined how supply chain management came into being as a response to a fundamental shift in the configuration of the production systems of companies driven by technological, competitive, demographic and financial pressures from around the early 1970s. Up to that point in time, companies tended to organize themselves as vertically integrated enterprises holding full ownership of many of the upstream and downstream components of their supply chain. Thereafter, in order to cope with the changing competitive environment, companies began to shift to a network model of production whereby they identified and focused on their core competences and obtained the other inputs and enabling services that they required from external suppliers and service providers. We also looked at some examples of companies such as Ryanair, Apple, Tesco and Walmart, which have successfully applied the concepts and tools of supply chain management over the last 35 years or so to create immensely strong and successful business models from small beginnings, and in doing so they realized that not only could they focus on optimizing their own core processes that lie within their direct control but also that they had to extend the system of interest to include the whole system of their suppliers and their suppliers' supplier to truly unlock the efficiencies that enabled them to create huge value and competitive advantage.

Finally, we looked at the important aspect of control and governance in these global production networks where there is a constant ebb and flow of influence and control between the lead players, the large producers and buyers, and the myriad suppliers and sub-suppliers in the network. While the dominance of the lead players may lead to the risk of abuse of that position of power, the smaller players can strengthen their position by proactively taking advantage of the requirement for the whole network to maintain stability and competitiveness for mutual benefit, This is achieved through cooperation, collaboration and joint action designed to deepen the complex interactions and relationships with other players in the network. Some of the key strategies that all companies can implement to unlock the advantages of supply chain management include focusing on core competences that they can clarify for themselves through identifying what the true driving force of their business is, while at the same time rationalizing and optimizing own supplier base and developing value-added, inter-organizational relationships and optimizing processes across these inter-organizational boundaries. By following these guidelines and relentlessly applying the insights, tools and techniques provide by supply chain management they can truly thrive, achieve sustainable success, and ensure that the whole is truly greater than the sum of its parts.

References

Dernbach, C (2018) Mac History: Apple I. Available from www.mac-history.net/apple-history-2/apple-i/2012-07-08/apple-i [last accessed 12 September 2018]

Ford Motor Company (2018) 100 Years of the Moving Assembly Line. Available from https://corporate.ford.com/innovation/100-years-moving-assembly-line.html [last accessed 4 October 2018]

Harvard Business School (2018) Netflix: the rise of a new online streaming platform universe. Available from https://digit.hbs.org/submission/netflix-the-rise-of-a-new-online-streaming-platform-universe/ [last accessed 4 October 2018]

Heckmann, P, Shorten, D and Engel, H (2003) *Supply Chain Management at 21: The hard road to adulthood*, Booz, Allen, Hamilton

Kepner-Tregoe (2018) Create a 'Strategic Culture' for successful implementation. Available from www.kepner-tregoe.com/pdfs/articles/Strategic-Response-2010-09.cfm [last accessed 4 May 2018]

Open University (2016) Systems Thinking and Practice (Kindle Edition). Available from www.amazon.com [last accessed 1 October 2018]

Philips, M and Ferdman, RA (2013) A brief, illustrated history of Blockbuster, which is closing the last of its US stores. Available from https://qz. com/144372/a-brief-illustrated-history-of-blockbuster-which-is-closing-the-last-of-its-us-stores/ [last accessed 12 October 2017]

Prahalad, CK and Hamel, G (1990) The core competence of the corporation, *The Harvard Business Review*. Available from https://hbr. org/1990/05/the-core-competence-of-the-corporation [last accessed 14 September 2018]

Ryanair (2018) History of Ryanair. Available from https://corporate.ryanair. com/about-us/history-of-ryanair/ [last accessed 5 August 2018]

Statista (2017a) Tesco's revenue worldwide in 2016/2017, by region (in million GBP). Available from www.statista.com/statistics/238678/ tesco-plc-group-sales-by-region-2010-2011/ [last accessed 25 June 2018]

Statista (2017b) Revenue value of Indian conglomerate Tata Group from FY 1996 to FY 2017 (in billion U.S. dollars). Available from www. statista.com/statistics/754924/india-annual-revenue-tata-group/ [last accessed 1 October 2017]

Statista (2018) Walmart's net sales worldwide from 2006 to 2018 (in billion U.S. dollars). Available from www.statista.com/statistics/183399/ walmarts-net-sales-worldwide-since-2006/ [last accessed 4 October 2018]

Waller, M (2013) How Sharing Data Drives Supply Chain Innovation, *Industry Week* (12/8). Available from www.industryweek.com/supplier-relationships/how-sharing-data-drives-supply-chain-innovation [last accessed 6 August 2017]

Womack, JP and Jones, DT (2005) *Lean Solutions: How companies can create value and wealth together,* Simon & Schuster, Sydney, Australia

Do you speak my language? 07
Supply chain communication

In this chapter, we are going to explore the importance of English as the international business language par excellence and additionally we are going to examine which other international languages may be significant for businesses that have their home base in English-speaking countries and who wish to develop business and supply chain relationships internationally. We will also see how important it is for businesses that internationalize their productive models and supply chains, whether that be from the point of view of sourcing overseas, selling into international markets or establishing their own production and distribution operations in other countries, to have a well thought out corporate language strategy that is both coherent in its formulation and implementation, and congruent with the business objectives of the company. Some companies may elect to have a single-language policy that dictates that one single language must be used always and everywhere for business matters, whereas others adopt a more nuanced approach that incorporates selective multi-lingualism depending on time, place and context. It is clear, however, that what will be highly detrimental to any business that ventures into international business without a clearly defined corporate language strategy is that default unfettered multilingualism will hamper both internal working relationships between colleagues in different countries as well as external supply chain relationships at the interface with key partners and stakeholders such as suppliers, service providers, distributors and customers potentially rendering these both inefficient and ineffective. Language can act as both a bridge or a barrier between people, between companies and between countries in different circumstances. We will touch on some of the pros and cons of adopting a single corporate language, usually English, and what the experience has been at those companies that have done so. We will also touch on how language proficiency both across different languages and within a given language, particularly in relation to developing a powerful vocabulary appropriate to the specific commercial circumstances, is so critical to success in every aspect of business.

English and other business languages

Since the end of the Second World War, English has increasingly become the international language of business. How did this come about? How did a language, that in the year 1500 was spoken by maybe 5 million people, on a relatively small island off the northwest coast of Europe come to be the lingua franca of the 21st century? Today, between 1.5 and 1.7 billion speak English as a first or second language in countries spread all over the world. That is almost one-quarter of the population of the planet. The real story of how English came to occupy this position of dominance is one of geopolitics and economic power. The French language had long been dominant in international affairs up until the 19th century and indeed it is still one of the most influential languages in international diplomacy. However, during the 18th and 19th centuries, a global British empire grew and was consolidated across the world and encompassing territories in North America, South and East Africa, the Indian subcontinent, Australia and Oceania. In the first half of the 20th century, particularly after the First World War, Britain's star began to wane, and the English-speaking United States emerged as the new global superpower. After the Second World War left many parts of Europe and East Asia in ruins, US economic, cultural and military power became dominant on the world stage and, along with it, the English language.

The Power Language Index

While the Power Language Index (PLI) developed by INSEAD's Kai L Chan (Chan, 2016) ranks English as the most influential language in the world today, there are of course other languages that are highly relevant in a business sense and that will be important for businesses large and small that internationalize their business models and develop global supply chain relationships. Chan's PLI looks to rank the global influence languages based on the following criteria:

- the ability to travel widely;
- the ability to earn a livelihood;
- the ability to communicate with others;
- the ability to acquire knowledge and consume media; and
- the ability to engage in diplomacy.

Based on these considerations, English is indisputably the most influential language in the world today and its score is twice as high as the second ranked language, Mandarin Chinese (Chan, 2016). The full top 10 ranked list of most influential languages is:

1 English
2 Mandarin Chinese
3 French
4 Spanish
5 Arabic
6 Russian
7 German
8 Japanese
9 Portuguese
10 Hindi

It is interesting to note that the projected top 10 ranking of the PLI for the year 2050 includes the same 10 languages but with some winners and losers in terms of which languages are predicted to rise in the rankings or increase their influence scores and which are projected to descend in the rankings. English is predicted to continue to be the most influential language in 2050 but with the distance between it and Mandarin Chinese, in second place, narrowed somewhat. Spanish will have risen in the rankings to substitute French as the third most influential language, with French dropping back to fourth place. Likewise, Portuguese will have jumped from ninth to eighth position and Hindi from tenth to ninth, having displaced Japanese from eighth position today to tenth in 2050. Arabic, Russian and German will maintain their relative ranking positions in fifth, sixth and seventh position. In short, English will remain dominant for the foreseeable future with Mandarin closing the gap a little. The biggest winners in relative terms will be Portuguese, Arabic, Hindi and Spanish and the losers will be French, Japanese, German and Russian.

Companies looking to expand their markets internationally would do well to note the languages of highest influence in the regions of the world in which they wish to do business, whether sourcing, selling or setting up operations, and to build their corporate language strategies accordingly. Those companies that aspire to become truly global in all major regions of the world may need to develop corporate language strategies that encompass many, if not all, of these most influential languages. The dominance of English as the global language of business has handed what appears to be a significant advantage to those who already have English as their mother tongue. In fact, some multinational corporations (MNCs), including some that do not have their origins in an English-speaking country, are adopting English as their single corporate language.

Despite the undoubted success of English among MNCs, more and more small- and medium-sized companies around the world are entering into international supply chain relationships as both customers of, and as suppliers to, businesses in other countries where English may not be spoken at all levels or where there is a need to interact with customers and consumers in an overseas market who do not share a common language with them. Regardless of the corporate language policy, proficiency in languages other than the native tongue of the enterprise lays a strong foundation at an individual level for the openness of mind, and the cultural attunement required to build and sustain successful international supply chain relationships required to reach both business clients and consumers with offerings that are appealing and compelling. Paradoxically, the fact that English has become the international language of business, it is precisely those whose mother tongue is English who may be at a disadvantage with regard to leveraging the benefits of language diversity in international business relationships. This is because a certain complacency may exist among native English speakers with an expectation that English will be valid in all international circumstances. Additionally, school-level language learning is not, generally speaking, a high priority in many of the larger English-speaking nations. This lower imperative to learn is then often coupled with a lower opportunity to learn in business and in personal interactions in which non-native English speakers prefer to practise their English when engaging with native English speakers rather than providing the English speaker the opportunity to engage in the local language.

The real stars in the field of diverse language acquisition are non-English speaking countries such as Germany, Japan, the Netherlands, Finland and others, where it is taken for granted that in business, proficiency in foreign languages including, but not limited to English, is a prerequisite for international business success. When we look at international trade we see that these countries have some of the highest proportions of their companies doing business overseas and it is part of the reason why they have been able to maintain healthy trade balances in their favour over long periods of time. Notwithstanding the fact that the United States is home to some of the most influential global businesses that the world has known – from Ford and GM in the early 20th century through to the likes of Apple, Google and Facebook today – it is quite astonishing to note that according to the United States International Trade Administration, of the 30 million or more companies that exist in America, fewer than 1 per cent of them export to markets outside the United States (ITA, 2018). This is well below the average for developed economies.

In contrast, in other English-speaking countries such as Canada and the United Kingdom, the percentage of companies exporting to overseas markets is about 10 per cent. These are still astonishingly low figures when it is considered that companies that export are consistently more profitable, more productive and more likely to stay in business longer than those that don't. More astonishing still is that with advances in transport services, supply chain management and financial services as well as developments in information and communications technology, it has never been easier or more economical to do business internationally.

The countries that have English as their main native language, often referred to as the Anglosphere, including the US, UK, Canada, Australia, Ireland and New Zealand, have a total population of native speakers of more than 400 million. Additionally, there is another group of countries in which the English language is official or co-official with other languages such as in India, Pakistan, Nigeria, South Africa and the Philippines. In these countries many people speak English as a first or second language and the population of people who have English as a second language exceeds 400 million. In addition to this, all around the world the number of people who can speak English but for whom English is a foreign language is approximately 650 million. Altogether somewhere in the region of 1.5 billion people, or almost a quarter of the population of the planet, can speak English competently.

In terms of international business, the languages other than English that are important and that are worthwhile developing as an internal capability will depend on several factors, including what areas of the globe your business interacts with, what type of commercial activity you are undertaking and where the country of interest is ranked on the EF English Proficiency Index (EF EPI). For example, if you are sourcing materials, that is buying, in central Europe where the native language is German and English language proficiency is generally high you could probably expect to conduct most business through English. However, if you are marketing or selling your products into these markets, either at a business-to-business or a business-to-consumer level, it is likely that you will need to be able to conduct business and provide materials in German.

The combination of economically important or rapidly developing areas of the world, combined with low English language proficiency in those areas indicates those languages that businesses working internationally, whether buying or selling, will need to develop competence in, whether that be for verbal interaction in day-to-day business, training, manuals, marketing materials, customer support or websites. For example, Russia is a large economy with specific strengths in sectors such as natural resources, engineering and IT, where English language proficiency is generally low. Likewise, Mexico, Colombia, Chile and Peru are open economies that are developing quickly and that provide many business opportunities. They are all Spanish-speaking countries and have generally low rankings on the EF EPI. Brazil is another important economic target for international business and is a Portuguese-speaking country with low levels of English proficiency in general. Many Arabic-speaking countries in the Middle East, French-speaking countries in Africa as well as China, have relatively low levels of English proficiency also.

Languages for international business

Some of the most important business languages for global operations and activities in the future besides English will be Spanish, German, Arabic, Russian, Mandarin Chinese, French and Portuguese depending on the area of interest and the business activities that are being undertaken. Spanish is a language that is on a growth trajectory within the United States, where it is the fastest growing linguistic group. There are currently 45 million first and second language Spanish speakers in the United States. Spanish is also the official language of several countries with largely developed or developing economies, including Spain itself, which is the fourth largest economy in the Eurozone with a GDP of $1.3 trillion and a population of nearly 49 million (CIA, 2018a). Spanish is spoken by over 400 million people worldwide. Mexico has the largest Spanish-speaking population in the world with some 125 million speakers and a GDP of $1.1 trillion (CIA, 2018b). Other significant Spanish-speaking countries include Colombia, with a GDP of $307 billion and a population of 48 million (CIA, 2018c) and Argentina with a GDP of $620 billion and a population of 44 million (CIA, 2018d). Mexico, along with Colombia, Peru and Chile, belongs to the economical dynamic Pacific Alliance and is particularly open to international business. The Pacific Alliance countries are on target to reach tariff-free trade between the members by 2020. Most of these countries, excepting Argentina where English language proficiency is high, rank moderate to low on the EF EPI, which indicates that businesses in the English-speaking world looking to establish strong supply chain links with the Spanish-speaking world will benefit significantly from the acquisition of the Spanish language as part of their business strategy.

French is a language with a glorious past as the international language of diplomacy that has declined in international importance in recent decades with the ascent of English but which is one that will likely see a new lease of life with the significant developments of economies on the African continent where French is spoken by many people as a first or second language. There is also the potential for French to gain importance again within Europe after the United Kingdom leaves the European Union in 2019. France itself is currently the second largest economy in the Eurozone, and in some respects bucks the population decline/stagnation seen in other large European economies such as Germany and Italy. France has a highly developed economy with a GDP of $2.5 trillion and a population of almost 65 million. Indeed, France's population is growing at twice the annual rate of Germany's and if current trends were to continue France's population would overtake Germany's before 2030.

There are some 220 million French speakers in the world. Apart from France, French is the main language or an official language in Canada and in many countries in Central and West Africa as well as in North Africa and in Madagascar in East Africa. French is also official in parts of the Caribbean, South America and Oceania. Of particular interest for the future are the developing African economies such as Morocco and Algeria in North Africa, as well as the two Congos, Gabon, Ivory Coast, Cameroon and others in sub-Saharan Africa, all of which speak French. These countries have growing populations and rapidly developing economies while at the same time having low or very low English-language proficiency. Consequently, English-speaking businesses with designs on developing business and supply chain links with these French-speaking countries should be looking at acquiring and developing French-language proficiency as an integral part of their business strategy.

Other languages that for similar reasons will be important to businesses in the English-speaking world to development, depending of course on their regions of interest and their activities in those regions, include Arabic, German, Portuguese, Russian, Japanese and Hindi. Arabic is official in 28 countries in North Africa and the Middle East and there are currently 245 million speakers. Notwithstanding the political instability and unrest in some of these, Arabic will be a useful medium for companies, particularly in the sectors of natural resources and security. German is spoken by 95 million native speakers mostly in central Europe in highly developed countries such as Germany, Austria and Switzerland, yet there are some 200 million speakers worldwide and German is particularly important in sectors such as science and technology. Portuguese has over 215 million native speakers in Portugal, Brazil, as well as Angola and Mozambique in Africa and is the fastest growing business language currently.

To develop an effective language strategy for your business, the key factors to consider are:

- the countries and regions of the world that you will be doing business with;

- the English-language proficiency rating of the countries of interest;

- the commercial activity will you be carrying on such as sourcing materials, products or services from the market or selling your own products or services into the market;

- the commercial business mode of operation, that is whether you will be operating in a business-to-business or a business-to-consumer mode;

- the language skills that you already possess within the organization – sometimes organizations are unaware of the full scope of language skills that their employees already possess;

- whether to develop internally or acquire by outside hiring of employees with further language skills; and

- the requirement for the use of professional external language and translation services, which can be of substantial value for the specialized technical translation of marketing material, for example technical manuals and instruction leaflets.

Translation and language acquisition

As with almost everything else in the modern world, the internet and the advances in information and communications technology are revolutionizing the world of foreign language teaching and acquisition and artificial intelligence is making some notable impact on the sector also. While currently artificial intelligence and neural networks are more of an aid to the human than a full-blown solution in themselves, it is possible that in time, with advances in machine learning these technologies may once again revolutionize the world of international communication. For example, Google's translation tool has been using artificial intelligence neural networks since 2016 (Matacic, 2016), which has increased the score on tests for its translation of texts from Spanish to English from 3.6 out of 6 to 5.0 out of 6, which is approaching the level of human translation which has a score of 5.1. Skype have also developed a simultaneous voice translation add-on for English to Spanish translation. However, these machine translation systems have their limitations still, not least of which is the limitation in the range of languages that they cover.

Some interesting resources that exist currently for language acquisition include:

- FluentU;
- italki;
- Duolingo;
- Babbel; and
- Memrise.

FluentU is a language learning app with a subscription-based model that is built around real-world video content with integrated quizzes and provides beginner through to advanced level material for a range of languages that includes Mandarin Chinese, Spanish, French, English, German, Japanese, Italian, Korean and Russian. FluentU also provides specialist English-language learning content for specific business sectors such as finance, technology, logistics, aviation and many more.

Italki is based on a person-to-person, student-to-teacher learning model using the power of internet video technology to connect learner and teacher from different parts of the globe in real-time lessons. Italki regards itself as a language learning social network. Italki provides a marketplace for language teachers, and students can choose from a wide range of professionally qualified language teachers on a commercial basis or they can engage in community type language exchange with people on a non-commercial basis. Italki has teachers who can provide tuition in over one hundred languages and while all the major languages are covered, italki can be particularly useful to find teachers in languages that may not be well covered by other language learning apps that are based on video, text or audio pre-recorded material. Languages that might fall into this category but that may be important for specific business requirements could be Indonesian, Malay, Turkish, Farsi or Hindi.

Duolingo is free language learning app that provides practice at progressive levels in a gamified format to test reading, writing and speaking skills. All the main languages are covered as well as several other languages that may be of interest for specific business needs such as Polish, Korean, Turkish or Vietnamese.

Babbel is a subscription-based app that focuses on interactive dialogue and prioritizes conversation and speaking skills. As well as covering all the major business languages discussed previously it also provides content on the languages of some of those larger up-and-coming economies such as Indonesian, Turkish, Polish and Russian.

Memrise is essentially a vocabulary-building app that provides content in an extremely wide range of languages as well as specialist topics within those languages. It is a highly gamified app in which memes and the user creation of memes is a central feature. These memes are leveraged to create unusual associations to help learners recall vocabulary more readily and efficiently.

These are all very useful resources for both individuals and for businesses and the selection of which app or apps to use will be dependent on the objectives of the language learning endeavour, as well as the learning style and learning priorities of the learner. Other more conventional CD and DVD-based courses such as those provided by Rosetta Stone, Linguaphone and Michel Thomas do still exist and these companies have also developed mobile apps and online multi-media options for language learners. Additionally, in every major town and city in the world these days there are language schools and academies that can provide standardized and tailored language learning experiences for business learners. These allow for businesses and language teaching service providers to craft personalized programmes for high potential corporate executives. For an international business today, the challenge is not so much one of access to learning options but rather one of knowing how to formulate and implement a corporate language strategy for itself with objectives that provide business value and ensure that the business will thrive in an international context where global supply chain relationships are the glue that hold together the frameworks that support the delivery of so many of the products and services that both businesses and consumers alike have come to expect in today's economy.

Corporate language strategies

When companies begin to trade internationally, whether buying, selling, setting up or acquiring operations abroad, they need to think about their strategy and policy for language competence and acquisition early in their international development. Many of course do not, and what can ensue thereafter is unnecessary cost, lack of speed and lost opportunity through miscommunication, lack of trust, loss of initiative in developing profitable lines of business, and underutilization of the resources of the business due to a lack of interoperability and flexibility across the business network. In some organizations that have operations spread across different countries, the unfettered multilingualism that can emerge organically by default in the absence of an explicit language strategy has led to this tragic sub-optimization of the resources and capabilities of the organizations and no little measure of frustration among employees, managers, supply chain partners and customers.

In one manufacturing company that I am familiar with where the home language was Spanish, international sales began in earnest when Spain joined the then European Community in the mid-1980s giving it freer access to other European markets and allowing the development of competences and capabilities that were then duplicated to secure business in other non-European overseas markets. By the early 90s, the company was exporting to the Middle East, East Asia, North and South America as well as to neighbouring European countries. The export department was set up with young, relatively inexperienced, junior-ranking people who could speak at least one second language, principally English, German or French, as well as the home language, Spanish. The head of this department, the youngest member of the management team, was the only member of management that could fluently speak English, or any other foreign language. None of the top management team, nor any of the directors or board members responsible for setting the strategic goals of the business, could speak any language fluently other than Spanish. Among the wider workforce of several hundred, the number of people that could conduct themselves competently in any language other than Spanish could be counted on the finger of one hand. The approach to language competency at the company could be described as, at best, tactical, reactive and minimalist. There was no overarching language strategy aligned to the goals and targets that the company had set itself for its international business nor with what the implication of achieving these goals would be for the employees and managers of the company as well as for the channel partners in the overseas markets. These channel partners, which included distributors, agents, resellers and, in time, wholly-owned subsidiaries and the individuals who worked with these channel partners, with the exception of those in Latin America, were all non-Spanish speaking nationals of the countries in which they operated.

The day-to-day impact of the absence of an overarching corporate language strategy included the following:

- An inordinate amount of non-value-added time was spent translating quotation requests from the channel partners in the international markets from English, French and German into Spanish so that they could be understood by the technical department who carried out the calculations and costings of the designs for the proposals and quotations.

- Likewise, additional time was spent translating the output of the technical departments for the proposals and quotations from Spanish into French, German and English before they could be sent to the channel partners for presentation to the clients and even in some instances thereafter in certain markets in Asia the channel partners needed to translate the proposals received in English from the plant in Spain to the local language, before it could be presented to the customer.

- All interaction between the top executives of the company and non-Spanish speaking executives who were customers or channel partners, required the presence of an interpreter, inevitably drawn from the small team at the export department. No negotiation, decision or exchange of written documentation for formal agreements could be completed without going through this laborious process of translation and interpretation.

- The number of people that could travel overseas in representation of the business to develop markets and interact with customers and channel partners was limited to a very small group and both the channel partners and the wider workforce in the technical and manufacturing departments felt disconnected and remote from each other and this remoteness as a retarding factor in the cementing of relationships of cooperation and trust because people could not converse easily in a direct manner.

This is an example of what can happen when a company does not view language as a strategic competitive factor in its international business ambitions but rather as a mere tactical and functional skill or competence to be acquired by individuals at a low level within the business. The negative business consequences of this approach are inefficiency, lack of responsiveness and an inability to fully exploit all the capabilities of the network of people within the business, at the channel partners and within the customer's businesses – in short, lower sales, higher costs and lower productivity than would other-wise be the case if these pitfalls had been effectively avoided with a corporate language strategy that was both coherent across the entire network and congruent with the strategic goals of the organization.

Today, more and more companies are coming to realize that they cannot afford to take a minimalist approach to their international corporate language strategies nor can they afford the costs and sub-optimization associated with unstructured multilingualism across their international networks. Consequently, it has become more and more common for companies to develop fully-thought-out and adequately resourced corporate language strategies. Some, like the Japanese electronic commerce and internet company Rakuten, headquartered in Tokyo, have adopted what from the outside might look like an extreme corporate language strategy by mandating English as their sole corporate language, even at home in Japan. In effect, they have changed the default language of the organization from the home language of Japanese to English. Other organizations, such as IBM, have adopted a corporate language strategy that is more nuanced and includes English as well as eight other languages. I am not arguing that one or other of these strategies, or any other, is superior, but rather that what companies need to do is to develop and implement explicit corporate language strategies that are coherent and congruent with what their own specific business requirements and goals are. Rakuten and IBM are very different organizations with very different business goals and cultures and consequently they have implemented very different corporate language strategies. However, what they both have in common is that they have not left the development of language competency across their international corporate network to chance, but rather they have thought through their goals and ambitions and have derived from these what their objectives should be and as a result they have developed and implemented consistent policies across their international networks to achieve those specific objectives.

The global English strategy

At Rakuten, the goal of the CEO, Hiroshi Mikitani, for the corporate language strategy was that every person who worked for the company, anywhere in the world, including the home base in Japan, would be able to demonstrate English language competence against an internationally recognized standard (Neely, 2013). Being a global internet company, the benefits that the company sought by pursuing this very ambitious goal was to be able to easily hire the best and the brightest from all over the world to increase the diversity of the company, which Mikitani felt would be a competitive advantage for a young company with global ambitions in the internet retail space. One effect of the adoption of the single language policy based on English, which Rakuten have rather awkwardly baptized "Englishnization" is that it enables non-Japanese speakers to progress and be promoted within the organization than would be common among Japanese-owned corporations. Indeed, Rakuten is unusual among corporate firms headquartered in Japan, in that over 20 per cent of its staff at the Tokyo headquarters are non-Japanese and 20 per cent of its executive officers are non-Japanese also (Neely, 2013).

This is a clear manifestation of a business globalization strategy that Pankaj Ghemawat of IESE Business School in Barcelona referred to in his article in the *Harvard Business Review* 'Managing Differences: The central challenge of global strategy' (Ghemawat, 2007) as an *Aggregation* globalization strategy, that is, an attempt to create standardization across a network of globally dispersed operations to leverage economies of scale and synergies with maximum flexibility to hire, deploy and promote people across that network. Other organizations, after analysing their business goals, develop alternative strategies. Ghemawat puts forward a framework of three distinct strategies for global operations. In addition to the Aggregation Strategy already mentioned, there is the Adaptation Strategy and the Arbitrage Strategy. In the Adaptation Strategy, the organization globalizes based on country-focused operations that adapt themselves to local requirements, tastes and customs. Companies such as IBM and others initially expanded globally in this fashion. Such a globalization strategy would likely lead an organization to adopt a language strategy in which a main corporate language, most likely English, would be adopted in conjunction with several other languages corresponding to the most important global business languages spoken in the locations and regions in which the company has operations. Typically, this would include languages such as Spanish, French, German, Portuguese, Chinese, Japanese, Arabic and others.

Many people working in front-line roles within country operations would not necessarily need to have a command of a language other than the language spoken in that country. However, beyond a certain level of management, in roles where people are required to interact with colleagues in other countries on joint projects or to engage actively in the cross-pollination of best practices it is likely that a good level of competence in English would be required. In high-level management, it is typical that to progress to the level of plant, site or country manager in this type of organization it will be a requirement for high-potential executives to take up management roles in other countries. To be most effective in this respect, managers may be required to have competence in one or two additional languages besides English.

Unfortunately, we still see cases of native Anglophone executives managing operations in countries such as China, Brazil or Mexico, where their limited competence in the local language forces them into a form of management isolation bubble, unable to interact directly with many of their people and unable to truly tap into the pulse of the business in the country or indeed to the society around them. In more recent times, with advances in the sophistication of supply chain management tools coupled with developments and innovations in technology, transport and finance many of the most advanced firms have begun to adapt globalization strategies that correspond to what Professor Ghemawat calls an Arbitrage strategy. In this type of arrangement, the organization looks to carry out different activities such as research and development, materials sourcing, primary and secondary manufacturing, assembly, distribution, sales and finance in different parts of the world to take advantage of specific arbitrage opportunities in labour, tax rates, subsidies, regulation and so on in different jurisdictions. These corporations become very complex interconnected networks with operations spread over the globe but collaborating and interacting in a continuous fashion, and in very coordinated and sophisticated ways.

This calls for a high degree of effective communication across international language and communications barriers on an ongoing and continuous basis. In effect, people at all levels within the businesses operations in different countries must interact with colleagues overseas on a day-to-day basis. Consequently, the requirement for a mandated corporate language will be high in companies with this type of globalization strategy. That corporate language will often be English even when the home language of the organization is not English. Clearly, it is critical to align the language strategy of the organization with the wider business strategy and the type of global configuration and requirements that the organization has.

Language competence definition and measurement

Competence in second-language acquisition is measured using the Common European Framework of Reference (CEFR) for languages. This framework was originally set out by the Council of Europe to provide a method for assessing language competence for all the languages of Europe. The CEFR is now becoming increasingly recognized as a global standard of assessing language competence. In the US, there are scales with equivalences to the CEFR such as the American Council on the teaching of Foreign Languages (ACTFL) proficiency guidelines and the Interagency Language Roundtable (ILR) scale. The CEFR classification of language proficiency assessment is based on six grades or standards across four separate key competences. The key competences are speaking, writing, listening comprehension and reading comprehension. The six standards are A1, A2, B1, B2, C1 and C2 and define competence broadly as follows (Council of Europe, 2001):

- A1 Beginner
- A2 Elementary Competence
- B1 Intermediate
- B2 Upper Intermediate
- C1 Effective Operational Proficiency
- C2 Mastery or Full Proficiency

To work effectively at a sophisticated level of business management working through a non-native language, a level of proficiency equivalent to CEFR C1 across all the key competences of speaking, writing, listening comprehension and reading comprehension would be required to command the structures and vocabulary needed to deliver sufficient intellectual firepower to communicate effectively with precision of meaning and expression in all circumstances. However, depending on a person's role, responsibilities and day-to-day activities, the level of proficiency across the four key competences may vary. For example, a person involved in the day-to-day coordination of international transport shipments requiring a lot of telephone interaction with colleagues in other jurisdictions may need a C1 level in listening comprehension and speaking but a B2 level in writing and reading comprehension might be sufficient. Conversely, a person working in a technical department that needs to interpret technical documentation and manuals but who has little direct verbal interaction with colleagues, suppliers or customers in other countries may require a higher level of competence in reading comprehension and writing, say a C1, whereas a B1 or B2 level in speaking and listening comprehension may not be an impediment to the effective execution of their work-related duties. Anecdotally, I can attest to the fact that when I worked with a manufacturing company in Spain as a young engineering technician during the 1980s and 1990s, I had many Spanish colleagues who worked in engineering and IT who were very comfortable dealing with written English in the form of manuals and technical books but were unable to maintain any kind of fluid conversation in English. The point here is that, in order for you as business owners and managers not to waste time, effort and money on unfocused and inappropriate language training, it is important that in the execution of the corporate language strategy appropriate and relevant training is provided in the key competences that actually matter for execution of the various functional roles across the organizational network.

Lastly, whatever our native language, most likely the one that most of us use in the greater part of our business interactions, business professionals operating at the highest levels in international business cannot afford to rest on their laurels in complacency with respect to the skills of understanding and expression in their own tongue. We all still need to improve our native language skills every day, our command of vocabulary and correct grammar as well as skilled expression in order to convey contextually appropriate and nuanced meaning to our co-workers, our customers and our suppliers, as well as to society at large in the form of the media or the general public. Success in business is about the quality of the relationships that we build and maintain to create and deliver value, and relationships are about effective communication and in human communication, despite much of the overblown hype and nonsense that we hear about the importance of body language, verbal language is the absolute king.

Summary

In this chapter, we have explored how English has become the most influential language in global business in the 21st century. This dominance grew through the 19th and 20th centuries, first through the extensive British Empire and then through the projection of economic, military and military power of the United States.

We have also pointed out that while English is and will continue to be the most influential business language in global business, a number of other languages are highly influential in certain regions of the world and in particular domains of competence and as a consequence businesses that have or that aspire to have truly internationalized business models will need to think very carefully about the formulation and execution of their corporate language policies. We have touched on how organizations such as the Japanese internet firm Rakuten and IBM have developed and implemented different corporate language strategies as a reflection of the requirements of their global business strategy and the structure of their business units across the globe.

While the top 10 most influential business languages in the world will remain the same through 2050 according to Kai L Chan's Power Language Index (Chan, 2016), the relative positions will switch around to some degree. English will remain at the top of the list and Mandarin will grow in importance. While Portuguese, Spanish, Arabic and Hindi will gain in influence, languages such as French, Japanese, Russian and German are projected to lose influence.

A key point to note is that, as was the case with Rakuten and IBM, corporate language strategy policy cannot be ignored and left to chance if organizations aspire to develop international and global business models that are both effective and efficient. In effect, companies must develop and implement corporate language strategies and policies are congruent with their wider business strategy and goals, coherent across the whole organization at all levels and appropriate to the tasks and responsibilities of individual functions. If this is not undertaken as an explicit policy, the likelihood is that a chaotic multi-lingualism will emerge across the international organization in which people will not be able to realize their full potential for the business, leading to frustration, ineffectiveness and inefficiency.

While the professional leverage is undoubtedly higher for speakers of one of the lesser global business languages such as Chinese, Spanish or French learning English than for an English-speaker to learn one of the lesser languages, in a global organization, a native English-speaker who acquires a high level of competence in one of the other influential business languages such as Mandarin, Spanish, Portuguese and so on can be a very powerful asset in a global business as can a speaker of one or more of those languages who acquires a high level of competence in English.

Whatever language we are using, and whether we are working through a language that is our native tongue or otherwise, we all need to continuously develop and improve our command of vocabulary, grammar and expression when aspiring to operate at the highest level in global business in order to be able to make ourselves understood so that we can contribute, influence and lead our businesses effectively so that they can continue to thrive in the future.

References

Chan, Kai L (2016) Power Language Index, Which are the World's most Influential Languages 30/05. Available from: www.kailchan.com [last accessed 23 May 2018]

CIA (2018a) The World Factbook (Spain), available from www.cia.gov/library/publications/the-world-factbook/geos/sp.html [last accessed 8 June 2018]

CIA (2018b) The World Factbook (Mexico), available from www.cia.gov/library/publications/the-world-factbook/geos/mx.html [last accessed 8 June 2018]

CIA (2018c) The World Factbook (Colombia), available from www.cia.gov/library/publications/the-world-factbook/geos/co.html [last accessed 8 June 2018]

CIA (2018d) The World Factbook (Argentina), available from www.cia.gov/library/publications/the-world-factbook/geos/ar.html [last accessed 8 June 2018]

Council of Europe (2001), Common European Framework of Reference for Languages: Learning, Teaching and Assessment (CEFR). Available from www.coe.int/en/web/common-european-framework-reference-languages [last accessed 15 February 2018]

Ghemawat, Pankaj (2007) Managing Differences: The central challenge of global strategy, *Harvard Business Review*, available from https://hbr.org/2007/03/managing-differences-the-central-challenge-of-global-strategy [last accessed 2 October 2017]

International Trade Administration (2017) About ITA. Available from www.trade.gov [last accessed 31 October 2017]

Matacic, Catherine, (2016) Google's new translation software is powered by brainlike artificial intelligence, available from www.sciencemag.org/news/2016/09/google-s-new-translation-software-powered-brainlike-artificial-intelligence [last accessed 1 February 2018]

Neely, Tsedal, (2013) Language and Globalization: 'Englishnization' at Rakuten (A), available from www.hbs.edu/faculty/Pages/item.aspx?num=40849 [last accessed 10 April 2018]

Babbel, available from www.babbel.com/

Duolingo, available from www.duolingo.com/

FluentU, available from www.fluentu.com/

Italki, available from www.italki.com/home

Memrise, available from www.memrise.com/

Right stuff, right 08
place, right time
Supply chain coordination

Effective supply chain relationships lead to successful supply chain operations. Product development and design, manufacturing, transport, warehousing, inventory management distribution and retailing – in a modern supply chain these operations cross departmental, organizational and national boundaries. The effectiveness of your day-to-day operations will be directly impacted by the quality of the relationships at these boundary interfaces, as will your ability to conceive, plan and implement innovative operational solutions to real-world challenges and achieve competitive advantage over competing supply chain configurations on the international stage.

Getting it there

Every company approaches the internationalization of its business in its own unique way, some by vocation and others by necessity; some build their international presence incrementally from their home base while others are born global. Whatever the ways and means your business adopts to take advantage of the huge opportunities of internationalization, ultimately, you must put in place the systems, processes and resources to ensure that the necessary materials, information and finance will be in the right place at the right time and in the right quantity to deliver consistently the desired business outcomes of service, quality and profitability. If you can do this effectively even as the international situation regarding geopolitics, economics and trade relationships evolves your business will grow and prosper. To do this well requires a broad range of skills and knowledge to research and evaluate the options, develop the supply chain design concepts, to implement the chosen solutions and to sustain and monitor their performance over time. Invariably this involves interaction and relationship building with a host of international stakeholders, some of whom will become critical strategic partners for the future success of your business. In the early years of the 20th century several large corporations, mostly American, began to internationalize their businesses in various ways. Chief among these were companies such as Singer, Westinghouse, Standard Oil, Eastman Kodak and General Electric (New American Nation, 2018). Some of the early motivations of this internationalization of American business were to do with saturated consumer markets at home, as well as the desire to secure supplies of critical materials such as oil, bauxite or rubber. In the decades after the Second World War, many other businesses from the economies of the more developed nations of Europe and North America also began to internationalize their businesses in earnest. This coincided with a time of improving communications, transportation technology and the dismantling of trade barriers and financial regulations that had been put in place during the conflictive decades of the 20th century, from the time of the First World War through to the end of the Second World War.

As companies gained experience and insight into doing business internationally, their perspectives and motivations changed and several different models for internationalizing evolved and developed. Companies began to realize that not only could they secure supplies and access high-potential overseas markets but that they could also diversify their overall risk by having operations and markets in many regions of the world. As they internationalized they realized that they could strategically place activities in locations that had comparative competitive advantages due to factors such as lower labour rates, tax levels and regulation. The coming together of all these factors gave rise to the emergence of the interconnected global supply networks that are such a feature of today's economy.

Developing countries are internationalizing

Over the last 20 years or so, those countries that were the receivers of a large part of the Foreign Direct Investment (FDI) that resulted from the internationalization of business, such as China, Taiwan, India and Mexico, began to develop international companies that became multinational companies themselves. Companies such as Tata, Acer, Lenovo and Grupo Carso from countries such as India, China and Mexico. Additionally, several smaller businesses, in response to both the threats and opportunities that the confluence of improving technology, reduction in trade barriers and the increase in customer desires and expectations provided, began to emulate the bigger companies and to internationalize in greater and greater numbers. Indeed, the United Nations Conference on Trade and Development (UNCTAD, 2018) indicates that there were about 7,000 multinational corporations active at the end of the 1960s whereas by 2006 just prior to the Great Recession this number had increased to the order of 80,000. While maybe 300 of these are very large organizations, there are now many, many companies all around the world, many of them classified as SMEs, that have internationalized their businesses in myriad ways and are reaping the benefits of their own strategies while adapting their approach as the international and global conditions change and evolve.

Internationalization strategies

Typically, the journey to becoming a company that trades internationally is an evolution that commences with the export of products or services to other countries within the company's home region. Indeed, the vast bulk of international trade and foreign direct investment is still intraregional. Typically, 60 to 70 per cent of international trade and investment happens within regions such as Western Europe, North America and Asia (WTO, 2017). This exporting endeavour inevitably brings the company into contact with new stakeholders and strategic partners such as international logistics operators, trade finance banking, customs and excise as well as agents and distributors in the target markets. This exposure is a fertile learning environment and one that drastically changes the outlook and strategy of the business. It is also an experience that presents company management with some very important decisions and challenges regarding how to move things forward. Should the company continue with an international strategy that is an export-only model or should it embark on more ambitious and aggressive international strategies based on franchising, licensing, joint ventures or the setting up of wholly-owned subsidiaries? Each company will develop its own tailored solution as a mix of these fundamental strategies.

Franchise model

The franchising model is one that has been successful for many companies in the food and retail business. World-famous fast food brands such as McDonald's, Burger King, Subway and KFC, which epitomize the franchising model, have internationalized based on this model. Other examples abound in sectors such as hotels, commercial cleaning, gym fitness, automotive repair, car rental and many others. Businesses that have operations that can be codified and systemized to provide a consistent output and quality can be particularly suited to the franchise model. The essence of the franchising model is a contractual relationship between the franchisor who owns the brand and the franchisee who owns and operates one or more outlets of the business in a locality or region. The franchisor provides the business operating system, the brand and ongoing support. This support can be very broad ranging and include site selection and development, operating manuals, training, brand standards, quality control, marketing strategy and business advisory support. Other types of franchising that are not so visible on the high street, yet generate a higher overall business volume, are product distribution franchising and manufacturing franchises. In manufacturing franchises, a manufacturer grants a franchisor the right to manufacture and sell goods using its trademarks and brands. Manufacturing franchises are common in the food and beverage manufacturing sectors.

In terms of an international expansion strategy, the franchising model offers some key benefits to the franchisor. Chief among these is the ability to enter markets without large capital investments in premises and equipment. Additionally, the franchisee brings local expertise, knowledge and alignment with the local culture and way of doing things, which the franchisor would find difficult to acquire rapidly. The international franchise model can be a way for franchisors to access growth opportunities rapidly in overseas markets and diversify their business, while maintaining a high level of control of the brand and the quality of the product or service delivered in the market. Again, successful franchising strategies, especially when expanding overseas, are successful to the degree that the quality of the relationship between the franchisor and the franchisee is formed and maintained with a high degree of mutual understanding, trust and common interest. All the usual challenges of identifying and selecting the best candidates, carrying out due diligence, providing the training and operating manuals in local languages and establishing and operating the supply chain, are magnified when expanding overseas.

Distributor model

Another channel commonly used to access overseas markets is the appointment of a distributor in the target market. Generally, distributors are established local businesses with a proven track record in the commercialization of similar products and services in their markets. As established businesses, these distributors can provide a ready-made route to market with an extensive customer base, knowledge of the local business culture and regulations and expertise in your specific business sector. They will be able to effectively promote and market your products through their existing sales and marketing capabilities. The foreign distributorship model is one that is very commonly used by companies that manufacture machinery and other equipment in business-to-business trading, particularly where there is a requirement for installation, maintenance and other types of after-sales services that the distributor can provide locally. For example, the storage equipment business that encompasses such products as pallet racking, shelving, mezzanine floors and their accessories is one that is now dominated by a small number of large manufacturing groups such as the Norwegian-owned Constructor Group and the

Barcelona-based Mecalux Group. In the past, this industry was far more fragmented, with many own-brand manufacturers such as Link 51, Stow and Esmena manufacturing in countries such as the United Kingdom, Belgium and Spain competing against each other around Europe, for the most part through appointed distributors with exclusivity for the products they distributed in their home countries, or within certain regions of their home countries. This enabled these medium-sized companies to project their brands across the continent of Europe, something that they would not have had the financial or operational capability to do with their own resources.

Nowadays, the European storage equipment manufacturing business has consolidated to a considerable degree with a good deal of manufacturing shifting to countries in Eastern Europe such as Poland, the distributor model perdures particularly in the smaller European countries. The reason for this is that the storage equipment business in each country is quite idiosyncratic, and dependent on very strong local connections and contacts. This diversity of market circumstances from country to country is combined with the fact that many national markets are relatively small, and the distributor, through representing a wide range of other related materials handling products such as conveyors, pallet wrappers, fork lift trucks and so on, is able to take on distributorship for multiple brands and provide viable access to the market that the storage equipment brand owner could not do based on their product range alone.

Additionally, these products require specialized installation teams, which are generally subcontracted locally. The local planning and coordination of this activity on a job-by-job basis is something that can be best coordinated at a local level by the appointed distributor company, who is also best placed to offer after-sales maintenance, repair and relocation services. Consequently, while the large manufacturing groups such as Constructor and Mecalux do now have wholly-owned subsidiaries operating under their brand names in some of the larger European countries, the distributorship model is one that will continue to be an important part of this and many other similar industries for the foreseeable future.

One of the advantages of the local distributor model is that it can provide rapid access to an unfamiliar foreign market without the need to develop the knowledge, contacts and know-how to operate successfully in that market. It also allows the exporting company to build up a familiarity with the business culture of the target market through its ongoing relationship with the local distributor company in an environment where both companies are incentivized to cooperate and to work together for mutual benefit. In some instances, depending on the success of the working relationship and the potential of the market, this distributorship model can become the foundation of a joint venture or acquisition by the exporting brand owner.

Of course, the main disadvantage of the distributorship model from the point of view of the brand-owning manufacturer is one of control. The local market distributor companies are independent businesses with their own brand and marketing presence. They own and control the interface and the relationship with the end users and therefore the brand owner is at a remove from the customers who acquire and use their products. As the brand owner's product range may be just one range of products within an offering including many others that the distributor represents, it can prove difficult for the brand owner in some instances to ensure that the distributor company and its sales team give priority and exposure to their products and their brand in the market. Consequently, it may take several attempts together with a lot of time, effort and perseverance to find the right distributor company in a market.

On the commercial front also, the distributor model presents several challenges. In effect, the distributor company purchases the products from the brand owner at a discount from the list price and resells them in its own name to local end users. The brand owner's credit risk for that entire market is therefore concentrated in just one company, the distributor, rather than being spread across all the end user companies as would be the case if the brand owner were dealing directly with these. To minimize credit risk, brand owners, particularly at the commencement of distributorship arrangements, will often insist on letters of credit or upfront payments before they will ship product to the distributor. This can put a working capital and cash flow burden on the distributor that can limit the speed and efficiency with which the distributor can ramp up the introduction of the brand owner's product range into the local market. Over time, as the working relationship and the mutual trust and familiarity grows, and the distributor company demonstrates a track record of sales and payment, some of these requirements can be relaxed, with the brand owner allowing credit terms to the distributor. In some cases, particularly on large single sales or projects where the sums of money involved exceed the financial capacity of the distributor company, the distributor may choose to act as an agent on commission, allowing the brand owner to complete the commercial deal with the end user company with the distributor providing coordination, quality control, delivery and installation services locally.

Joint ventures

The Spanish have a neat expression 'estamos juntos pero no revueltos', which translates loosely as something like 'we are together but not in each other's pockets', which is an apt description of the distributorship model discussed in the previous section. In this sense, the distributorship model allows for cooperation to achieve certain business goals and objectives that are mutually beneficial but without a joint commitment to a common business entity in the form of equity, debt or other forms of capital investment that constitute a shared or common ownership and the accountability that comes with that. In those instances where a greater level of control is essential to the brand owner or exporting company, or where a distributorship relationship has developed to a degree that both parties can see a financial benefit in pooling their resources to increase profit margins and efficiency, joint ventures can provide a mechanism that allows each partner to bring their complementary strengths to the endeavour to achieve business outcomes such as growth, profitability or market share that would not have been possible for either working alone or in collaboration through the classical distributorship model.

Typically, a joint venture is a separate business entity, most often a limited liability company, formed by two or more businesses, but distinct from each of these. The participating businesses agree to contribute assets such as premises, stock and equity, and they agree how profits, losses and management decision-making will be shared between them. In effect, the participating companies will be jointly responsible for the formulation and implementation of the strategy, policy and activities of the new business. As a strategy for doing business internationally, the joint venture brings the advantages of the distributorship model, that is, access to the knowledge, contacts and cultural alignment of a local partner in the market but at the same time it brings with it a level of financial and management control that is absent in the distributorship model. This can enable the company accessing the new foreign market to accelerate market penetration, ensure prioritization of their products and services, increase profitability, control quality and ensure brand promotion and recognition. The joint venture arrangement can also facilitate operational strategies that would be difficult to achieve through the distributorship model and that can improve service and responsiveness to market requirements. These can include the placement of stock inventory in the local market for rapid order fulfilment, localization of products within the market through carrying out assembly and packaging locally, thus reducing international transport volumes and costs.

Evidently, the level of trust, commitment and cultural alignment and awareness that is required to enter into and sustain a joint venture enterprise at an international level is considerable.

Wholly-owned subsidiaries

Some businesses opt to internationalize, whether initially or after passing through the distributorship, joint venture pathway, by setting up wholly-owned subsidiaries in overseas markets by means of foreign direct investment (FDI), where this is considered desirable, aligns with the business strategy and capability and is legally permissible. Indeed, some countries such as China, Brazil and UAE, require, or have required in the past, that foreign businesses form joint ventures with local parties to set up certain types of operations within their territories, thus precluding full foreign ownership of businesses within their borders. The great advantage of the wholly-owned subsidiary from the point of view of the foreign investing company is that in addition to the market access provided by the joint venture model, the wholly-owned subsidiary places full operational and strategic control of the business in the hands of the investing company. This can contribute to enhancing intellectual property security and guarding to some degree against IP theft and counterfeiting, which has become a serious issue in many sectors such as automotive parts that have internationalized their supply chains over the last couple of decades. Some of the disadvantages associated with wholly-owned subsidiaries is that the investing company takes on the full costs and implications of its foreignness, including the challenges with local hiring, and operational set-up, as well as establishing relationships with local vendors and suppliers. Additionally, the investing company takes the full investment risk for the enterprise. The wholly-owned subsidiary, albeit with varying forms and strategies of deployment, is the building block of the multinational and transnational corporations large and small that have become such a significant feature of the modern economy and the global supply chains and networks that connect their operations. Companies such as Ford, Starbucks, Disney and GSK are typical of such international businesses, as are some of the US conglomerates such as Time Warner, Alphabet and Kraft Heinz, the Japanese Keiratsu such as Mitsui, Mitsubishi and Sumitomo, as well as the South Korean Chaebol such as Samsung, Hyundai and LG.

Although the better-known multinational and transnational enterprises are very large businesses, there are also a great number of smaller businesses all around the world that also successfully conduct multinational operations. These constitute a far more relevant model for smaller- and medium-sized enterprises (SMEs) that are looking to internationalize their business. Take, for example, the veterinary pharmaceutical company Bimeda. The company was founded in Dublin Ireland in the mid-1960s and has grown to be a manufacturer, marketer and distributor of animal health products and veterinary pharmaceuticals with a turnover of €143 million in 2016 (Bimeda, 2018). Bimeda employs about 250 people in Ireland and a similar number outside Ireland. From its 10 manufacturing sites in 7 countries and 5 laboratories across 4 continents Bimeda serves markets in 75 countries and has either a manufacturing, commercial or distribution presence in Ireland, the UK, Canada, the US, Mexico, Brazil, Kenya and China.

Another example of a smaller scale multinational company is the Spanish storage and intralogistics solutions provider Mecalux. The company was founded in 1966 in Barcelona in a small workshop with the manufacture of simple steel shelving units. In the 1980s the company began to internationalize its business opening sales offices in France, the United Kingdom and Germany, and its first overseas production plant in Argentina (Mecalux, 2018). Today, Mecalux provides integrated materials handling and storage equipment solutions including automated storage and retrieval systems and the controlling software for warehouses and distribution centres and operates 11 production facilities around the world in Spain, Poland, the US, Mexico, Brazil and Argentina. The company now employs 3,000 people and has a turnover of more than €500 million.

These are just a couple of examples of companies from different sectors and different countries that have managed to navigate and negotiate their way to establish an internationally diversified footprint for their business from small beginnings and they illustrate the point that not all successful international businesses are mega enterprises and that other small- and medium-sized enterprises can emulate the success of these leaders.

Every business that internationalizes its activities follows its own unique path and the strategies that it deploys at different times in its evolution will tend to adapt both to its internal requirements and external forces such as international trade agreements, security considerations, currency fluctuations and geopolitics. Consequently, the configuration of a company's international activities at any point in time will be a hybrid model comprising combinations of wholly-owned subsidiaries, joint ventures, distributorships and other types of international strategic alliances. Nonetheless, these are several different models or strategies that are discernible in international business configurations. There is always a certain tension and balance that international businesses try to strike between centralized control for standardization and efficiency on the one hand versus local responsiveness and effectiveness on the other. Four different template models that are useful to consider when thinking about the international configuration of your business are the following:

- the cookie cutter model
- the autonomous markets model
- the relative advantage model
- the integrated model.

The cookie-cutter model

In the cookie cutter model international operations situated in different countries essentially provide the same standardized offering in all regions. As a result, the operational and strategic control of international operations tends to be highly centralized in this internationalization strategy. This model will be most appropriate when the offering itself is highly standardized and brand recognition is also very high. Automotive production, aerospace and telecommunications will often adopt this approach, whereby overseas operations are almost carbon copies of the home country operations in terms of processes, standards and outputs. Local operations are essentially executors of the plans and strategies developed at the centre and have minimal involvement in those activities. The standardization allows the company to leverage economies through scale, reduced complexity and maximum efficiency in optimum global locations. The focus at the local level is on efficiency, productivity and operational excellence in the face of highly commoditized and price-sensitive markets. Strategic decision-making, design, research and development and other high value and intellectual property creating activities are held at the centre in the home country. This is essentially a cost leadership strategy.

The autonomous markets model

In the autonomous markets model, product and service offerings require significant adaptation to local tastes and preferences and consequently the model is based on regional or national operations, each with a considerable degree of autonomy and alignment to the locality in which they are situated. Businesses in the food sector, personal and business services, and healthcare will often find that there is a very high requirement to adapt their offerings to local preferences. In this strategy, company subsidiaries in each country will enjoy a considerable degree of autonomy to formulate and implement their own business strategies while at the same time leveraging the power of the parent company regarding financial, marketing and logistics capabilities giving them a strong advantage over local firms. A good example of this approach is the International Airlines Group (IAG), which is the parent company of four distinct airlines – British Airways, Aer Lingus, Iberia and Vueling. On the IAG website (IAG, 2018) they describe themselves as: *'IAG combines leading airlines in Ireland, the UK and Spain, enabling them to enhance their presence in the aviation market while retaining their individual brands and current operations. The airlines' customers benefit from a larger combined network for both passengers and cargo and a greater ability to invest in new products and services through improved financial robustness.'* British Airways, Aer Lingus and Iberia are the three former national flag carriers of the United Kingdom, Ireland and Spain respectively, and while they all now all form part of IAG, each one still retains its own character and brand and the customer experience of flying with one or the other is clearly differentiated.

The relative advantage model

In this model companies seek to maximize location economies and to exploit relative advantage or arbitrage opportunities in labour, compliance or fiscal pressure in the configuration of their global value chains. Companies that adopt this strategy will often be those with globally recognized products and brands that differ little from place to place. Like in the cookie cutter model many of the high-end capabilities regarding intellectual property development, design, strategy and supply chain coordination are held at the centre while opportunities are sought to locate manufacturing and assembly in the most cost-effective locations. This strategy requires top-class logistics and supply chain systems design and implementation to ensure that cost, service and availability can be controlled for competitive advantage. If you own an Apple iPhone, look at the back cover and you will see printed there in small letters, 'Designed by Apple in California. Assembled in China' (Rawson, 2012). This is a clear indication that Apple's value chain has been configured in a manner that seeks arbitrage opportunities around the globe for different value chain activities, in this case, R&D in California, assembly in China. The fact that the successor to Steve Jobs as Chief Executive Officer is Tim Cook, Apple's former Chief Operating Officer and the person responsible for the design and implementation of Apple's global supply chain, is also testament to the fact that one of the keys to Apple's success is the quality of its supply chain and logistics capabilities that is essential for this type of value chain configuration to be successful.

The integrated model

As the complexity and the rate of change of the global economic and geopolitical situation increase over time, many companies find that they need to adjust their value chain configurations in more sophisticated ways to adapt locally where this is required, as well as to identify opportunities where global standardization can deliver business benefits and where their core competences can be used to leverage their competitive advantage globally across the whole value chain. The implementation of this type of strategy requires the organization to develop, maintain and nurture a very high level of skills and competences to ensure effective coordination, learning, communication, knowledge capture and dissemination, together with the leveraging of partnerships and strategic alliances across the globe.

Flexibility and future trends

Each of the models that we have discussed implies a different configuration of the value chain of the business, which itself is a product of the business strategy, and whether this is one of differentiation, as in the case of a high-end car manufacturer such as Lamborghini, as opposed to one of cost leadership as is the case of the low-cost airline Ryanair. The value chain concept developed by Michael Porter and described in his seminal book *Competitive Advantage* (1985) sets out how businesses create value through the various process steps in what he termed the value chain. Companies create value through the sequence of activities that directly produce the product or service, known as primary activities, together with the support activities that make the execution of the primary activities possible. Primary activities will include inbound and outbound logistics, operations, sales, marketing and service. The support activities are not directly involved in the production and delivery of the product or service but make these activities possible. The support activities include procurement, human resources management, IT, knowledge management and business administration and general management functions. Take, for example, a large pharmaceutical manufacturer with an end-to-end value chain that will typically stretch from primary manufacturing producing, say, an active pharmaceutical ingredient (API) to the secondary manufacturing layer where final products, such as capsules or tablets containing the API, are manufactured and packaged as finished product. These in turn are marketed and sold through the various layers of the wholesale and retail distribution channels.

All these activities are tied together by the various inbound and outbound logistics functions between primary manufacturing, secondary manufacturing, wholesale and retail. The importance of understanding how the business creates value and how this governs the choices about the location of these value-creating activities as the company begins to internationalize its activities and operations is critical because in essence, as Porter sets out, profits are the difference between the value that the company creates through its primary and support activities to make and deliver its products and services and the cost of creating those products and services (Porter, 1985). How the company decides to configure and coordinate its value chain to deliver its strategy is going to have a major impact on whether the company is profitable and thrives or is unprofitable and dies.

In practical reality, the configuration that any real business will adopt as it rolls out its international activities and operations will be a hybrid mix of the models that we have described, and one that will be in continuous flux in response to constantly shifting and evolving international economic, political, legal and cultural factors. These constantly changing factors impact greatly the internal decision-making processes related to where the various parts of the primary and support functions of the value chain are located and how the various elements are configured and coordinated. These changes can have significant impacts on strategic business outcomes such as cost, service and quality, and consequently must be constantly monitored and measured. The firm must be flexible and adaptable enough to reconfigure its value chain in line with its strategy and its driving force in response to the external environmental conditions. In effect, the configuration and coordination of its value chain must evolve and shape-shift as required, forming new international supply chain relationships so that the business can continue to thrive. The manifestation of this process of continuous change and reconfiguration has been seen clearly over recent decades as some companies have opted to offshore parts of their value chain to foreign locations that are very far away from the home country, sometimes through wholly-owned or joint venture arrangements. For example, many European OEM car manufacturers have set up in Eastern Europe and in China. Another example is illustrated through companies partnering with contractors and service providers in foreign locations such as Apple's partnership with the Taiwanese-owned Foxconn for the manufacture of the iPhone also in mainland China (Kanematsu, 2017). When this makes sense, sometimes it is to gain market access that would otherwise be closed or where a combination of cost arbitrage and logistics excellence means that the product can be produced in the distant offshore location and yet delivered to the consumer in the home markets in a cost-effective manner.

Other companies have chosen to adopt strategies that keep things much closer to home with a homeshoring approach. This is literally keeping all elements of the value chain physically located in the home country, as in the case of the Italian carmaker Ferrari where design, quality and reputation outweigh cost considerations. In other cases, we see onshoring strategies that involve keeping operations in the home country but looking for cost optimization through the location of some activities and operations in other parts of the home country where costs are lower or there are incentives or stimuli provided by regional, state or local authorities. For example, onshoring is a phenomenon that has been apparent in the US for some time as many manufacturing businesses have shifted operations from northern and north-eastern states where organized labour has pushed up costs relative to southern and south-western states that have become the recipients of the transfer of these activities.

Yet other strategies that have been adopted include nearshoring, where certain elements of the value chain are moved to neighbouring countries. For example, many US companies have shifted some operations across the border into Mexico and a similar pattern has emerged with Western European companies moving operations to Eastern European locations such as Poland, Czech Republic, Hungary and Romania.

Supply chain logistics

The more complex and sophisticated the value chain configuration of an international business, the more difficult will be the logistical challenge of managing the effective movement and positioning of resources such as inventory, information and finance and the coordination of related activities such as transport, materials handling, and customs clearance together with the utilization of key assets such as trucks, ships, factories and warehouses. Those companies that have developed levels of competence in global logistics and supply chain management such as Zara, Apple and Walmart, among others, aligned with their value chain configuration to enable their business strategies to be implemented effectively are those that have thrived in the modern economy.

While all companies form part of multiple supply chains in their different roles of supplier, customer or service provider, not all companies are practising supply chain management. We have discussed previously how the key distinction is that the practice of supply chain management involves a systems approach to the design, coordination and measurement of the value chain to optimize the overall organization as opposed to the traditional approach of each element of the business trying to optimize its own performance without regard to the wider organization. This is an approach that is increasingly recognized as being fundamentally dysfunctional and wasteful of resource, money and talent. Consequently, companies that are embarking on their international adventures, whatever form their value chain ultimately takes to best align with their strategy and the requirements of their customers, need to begin to think in terms of the overall organizational performance and to develop the skills and competences among their employees to enable them to formulate, implement and measure these configurations and solutions.

More and more companies are creating C-level roles for executives with responsibility for the end-to-end management of the supply chain. These new chief supply chain officers (CSCOs) are becoming key players in the success of the best managed companies in the world and indeed in 2016, Hans Thalbauer, Senior Vice President with SAP wrote, 'today the CSCO may be the most important role in the executive suite' (Thalbauer, 2016).

Key partners to many companies in the endeavour to effectively vertebrate and articulate their value chains will be key partner companies known as logistics service providers (LSPs). These are companies that have developed competences, capabilities and resources in transport, warehousing, forwarding and customs clearance on an international scale that allow them to provide a range of logistics services, in many instances customized to individual requirements to make possible the configuration and coordination of the complex value chain arrangements that we discussed earlier. These relationships between manufacturers and distributors and their logistics service providers are becoming longer in duration and more strategic in nature as the complexity of global supply chain configurations increase. The result of this is that the ability to effectively specify, implement, measure, sustain and improve working relationships with logistics services providers on an international scale is indispensable for any organization with ambitious international strategies. In addition to warehousing, transport and freight forwarding services, logistics services providers are increasing developing capabilities to provide further value-added services to their customers that include the following:

- merge in transit
- stock consolidation
- crossdocking
- pick and packing of orders
- procurement
- inventory management
- localization and labelling
- packaging and assembly
- supplier management
- sampling and quality control
- trade regulation and customer compliance
- security
- insurance.

The larger logistics services companies have become multinational corporations themselves and are able to provide economies of scale and economies of scope to customers across the globe in sectors in which they have developed specific competence. According to the supply chain research and consultancy company Armstrong & Associates in 2015 (Armstrong and Associates, 2015) the top 10 logistics service providers in the world and their annual revenue in millions of US dollars were:

1 DHL (27,562)

2 Kuhne & Nagel (21,100)

3 DB schenker (17,160)

4 Nippon Express (15,822)

5 C.H. Robinson (13,476)

6 UPS (8,215)

7 DSV (7,574)

8 Sinotrans (7,314)

9 CEVA Logistics (6,959)

10 Expeditors (6,617)

Future trends

As noted earlier, the economic and geopolitical environment governing the decision-making processes regarding the configuration of global operations undergoes continual change. Another area of constant change and advancement that is also impacting these decisions is that of technological innovation and the digitalization of industry that is sometimes referred to as Industry 4.0. This embraces the convergence of several technologies including robotics, additive manufacture, cloud computing and the internet of things. This is giving rise to radical new options in the configuration of value chains as well as making possible the emergence of radical new digital-platform-based business models, some of which are proving to be extremely disruptive to incumbent market leaders in several business sectors.

Additive manufacture/3D printing

Advances in 3D printing technology from companies such as Hewlett Packard and EOS are bringing industrial-scale additive manufacture and 3D printing into focus as a viable and competitive option for many companies in the automotive, aerospace and medical devices industries, among others. Several different additive manufacturing technologies currently exist including laser sintering for metals and photopolymerization for plastics. With this technology, the economics of the production of certain products and components can be literally turned on its head. The need to manufacture large runs in far-off locations to achieve economies of scale is no longer required. Inventory in effect can become virtual, with the files for parts stored digitally and printed on demand in small quantities without the need for retooling. Production can be delayed until products are required, the point of production can be brought closer to the point of use and the component materials remain in their generic format until they are finally printed. All these advantages have major implications for the location of manufacturing facilities, transport, logistics, inventory management and working capital, and will likely have a significant impact on supply chain design in certain sectors in the future.

Robotics

Industrial robots have been deployed for several decades across many industries, most notably in the automotive sector, which is still the biggest user of industrial robots. These robots have been performing tasks such as welding, forming, riveting and so on. Indeed, by 2016, there were some 1.8 million industrial robots installed across the world with countries such as the US, China, Japan, South Korea and Germany leading the way in terms of new installations (International Federation of Robotics, 2017). Generally, these machines have been large and fast and need to be deployed with comprehensive safety measures such as fences and barriers to protect human operators from injury thus limiting their utility to certain heavy-duty processes. However, the new generation of robots that are coming on stream now include a new generation of sensor-enabled robots that can work on more complex tasks in proximity to human beings in a safe manner. These machines are called cooperative robots or cobots. The sensors in these machines allow them to adjust their movements to take account of the presence and movements of human beings in close proximity. Additionally, through machine learning and machine vision, they can learn to perform complex tasks that heretofore were outside the realms of application of robotics. Consequently, we are beginning to see the advent of mobile collaborative robots or intelligent integrated work assistants (iiwa) that can move freely around a facility such as a factory or warehouse and perform activities such as order picking, packing, replenishment, assembly and so on (KUKA, 2018). With the cost of these robots decreasing to levels that make them both affordable and scalable for small- and medium-sized companies, the potential for deployment in traditionally labour-intensive activities in warehouse operations, and production lines that were previously nonviable is becoming an ever more realistic proposition.

Internet of things and big data

With the proliferation of sensors that are being incorporated into every type of manufactured product, together with cloud computing and the possibility of every individual item having its own IP address through the adoption of IPv6, the new internet protocol which provides for 340 undecillion internet addresses, that is 340 trillion-trillion-trillion (Search Enterprise, 2010). These IP addresses allow each item's location and identification to be defined. With so many devices connected to the internet, the possibility of collecting and analysing enormous quantities of data expands to unprecedented levels, making it possible to optimize manufacturing processes, streamline supply chain configurations, optimize inventories and monitor and manage operational performance to the item level in a manner that has never been possible before.

Blockchain technology

With the interconnection of multiple systems and things of all types, the existence of IP in digital formats, together with sensitive and valuable data on digital platforms, the risks associated with malicious cyber attacks for the purposes of blackmail and extortion, counterfeiting, pirating and fraud also increase dramatically. People and businesses will need technologies to help them to have trust in the processes, products and services. One of the technologies that will be significant in this regard will be blockchain technology.

Essentially, a blockchain is a distributed database composed of a succession of interconnected blocks with time stamps that constitute a single source of truth for a succession of events, records, activities or transactions (Kharpal, 2018). This technology has significant potential in the certification and validation supply chain activities that take place across inter-organizational boundaries as is typical with the myriad configurations of value chains in today's global economy. Indeed, in 2016 the *Irish Times* printed a story (Taylor, 2016) that the Irish dairy products company and owner of the Kerrygold brand, Ornua, had completed what was believed to be the world's first global trade transaction using blockchain. According to the *Irish Times*: '*The letter of credit transaction between the group and the Seychelles Trading Company arose following a collaboration involving Barclays Bank and the Israeli start-up, Wave. The transaction is the first to have trade documentation handled on Wave's new distributed ledger technology platform, which has been designed to speed up transactions, cut costs and reduce the risk of fraud.*' Indeed, in January 2017, the World Economic Forum report predicted that that by 2025 10 per cent of global GDP will be stored on blockchains or blockchain-related technology.

Summary

In this chapter we have explored the various configuration and coordination strategies that organizations adopt to implement their international business operations and create value chains that align with their business strategy and their driving force to deliver the products and services that their customers want to purchase at prices that deliver sustainable profit margins. Each individual business approaches the challenges of internationalization in its own way. Some progress iteratively through the steps of direct export, distributorship, joint venture and wholly-owned subsidiaries while others, particularly in these days of digital platform business models, are literally born global. Whatever the road that is chosen or that unfolds for a company, the ability to view the value chain as a whole system with multiple components and stakeholders and to think about and measure its performance from that viewpoint is a key competitive differentiator in a world where a systemic approach to the management of the supply chain is the key competence that sets the best performing companies in the world apart from the rest. Several key points are noteworthy:

- All internationalization models require the ability to build and sustain long-term sustainable relationships across language and cultural boundaries with different legal and fiscal frameworks.

- The international configuration and coordination of the value chain needs to be in constant flux to adapt to the changing economic, geopolitical and technological environment.

- Top class logistics capabilities are essential to leverage the full potential of the various value chain configurations that are available.

- A highly developed global logistics services provision sector has developed in recent decades to provide the transport, warehousing, freight forwarding and other value-added services required by firms as they internationalize their business.

- Technological advances in the fields of additive manufacture, internet of things, big data and analytics, robotics and blockchain are set to have a dramatic impact on the configuration of international business models and physical operations in the future.

References

Armstrong and Associates (2015) A&A's Top 50 Global Third-Party Logistics Providers (3PLs) List. Available from www.3plogistics.com/3pl-market-info-resources/3pl-market-information/aas-top-50-global-third-party-logistics-providers-3pls-list/ [last accessed 5 November 2016]

Bimeda (2018) A Global Presence with Irish Roots. Available from www.bimeda.com/about/ [Last accessed 4 October 2018]

International Airlines Group (2018) about Us. Available from www.iairgroup.com/phoenix.zhtml%3Fc%3D240949%26p%3 Daboutoverview [Last accessed 25 July 2018]

International Federation of Robotics (2017) By 2020 more than 1.7 million new industrial robots will be installed in factories worldwide. Available from https://ifr.org/ifr-press-releases/news/ifr-forecast-1.7-million-new-robots-to-transform-the-worlds-factories-by-20. [Last accessed 3 October 2018]

Kanematsu, Y. (2017) Foxconn, Apple and the partnership that changed the tech sector. Available from https://asia.nikkei.com/Business/Foxconn-Apple-and-the-partnership-that-changed-the-tech-sector [last accessed 4 October 2018]

Kharpal, A (2018) Everything you need to know about the blockchain (CNBC 18/6). Available from www.cnbc.com/2018/06/18/blockchain-what-is-it-and-how-does-it-work.html [last accessed 4 October 2018]

KUKA (2018) LBR iiwa. Available from www.kuka.com/en-de/products/robot-systems/industrial-robots/lbr-iiwa [last accessed 1 October 2018]

Mecalux (2018) History. Available from www.mecalux.com/company/history [last accessed 2 October 2018]

New American Nation (2018) Multinational Corporations – Early multinational corporations. Available from www.americanforeignrelations.com/E-N/Multinational-Corporations-Early-multinational-corporations.html [last accessed 2 August 2018]

Porter (1985) *Competitive Advantage: Creating and sustaining superior performance*, Free Press, New York

Rawson, C. (2012) Why Apple's products are 'Designed in California' but 'Assembled in China'. Available from www.engadget.com/2012/01/22/why-apples-products-are-designed-in-california-but-assembled/?guccounter=1 [last accessed 5 June 2018]

Search Enterprise (2010) IPv6 (Internet Protocol Version 6). Available from https://searchenterprisewan.techtarget.com/definition/IPv6 [last accessed 2 October 2017]

Taylor, C (2016) Ornua involved in groundbreaking blockchain transaction. (*Irish Times* 7/9). Available from www.irishtimes.com/business/technology/ornua-involved-in-groundbreaking-blockchain-transaction-1.2782748 [last accessed 10 January 2018]

Thalbauer, H (2016) Is Chief Supply Chain Officer Most Important Role In Executive Suite? Available from www.forbes.com/sites/sap/2016/03/25/is-chief-supply-chain-officer-most-important-role-in-executive-suite/#2f1fa67123ee [Last accessed 2 October 2018]

UNCTAD (2018) Largest Transnational Corporations. Available from https://unctad.org/en/Pages/DIAE/World%20Investment%20Report/Largest-TNCs.aspx [last accessed 1 February 2018]

World Trade Organization (2017) Trade by Region. Available from www.wto.org/english/res_e/statis_e/tradebyregion_e.htm [last accessed 12 September 2018]

Finger on the pulse

Control and measurement

Measurement is critical to understanding how effective our solutions are at helping us to achieve our business objectives. However, measuring the performance of isolated components within a supply chain is not what is required. If the supply chain is a system, then we need to be able to measure its outputs and share that knowledge among the supply chain partners. This presents many challenges of coordination, transparency and trust, all these attributes that are forged in the crucible of the supply chain interfaces between the partners.

Control and governance

International supply chain relationships are a mixture of working arrangements, loose associations, legal contracts and informal understandings with myriad independent players – some, as we saw in Chapter 4, are longer-term, relatively stable arrangements with binding legal contracts and performance targets, while others, as we discussed in Chapter 5, are shorter-term and more fluid alignments that form, dissolve and reform as required. Add to this the complexity of the international element, which brings with it differences in language and culture, as well as very different legal and fiscal frameworks between jurisdictions, then one begins to appreciate that the control, governance and measurement of what is really happening is a special challenge indeed.

In addition, each one of the independent players in these arrangements will be involved in other similar arrangements in separate supply chains and will therefore be subject to other competing agendas and priorities. The issue of confidentiality, security and the protection of sensitive information and data is yet another element to be taken into consideration. There are many different supply chain models in existence, some supply chain configurations are driven by the peculiarities and structure of certain industrial sectors and others are the result of purposeful strategic design and configuration on the part of lead organizations.

One supply chain that is very much conditioned by the environmental factors on one hand and by historical legacy on the other is the supply chain for natural diamonds. The environmental factors that dominate the structure of the supply chain is that the sources of natural diamonds are limited to certain regions of the planet. Indeed, 65 per cent of the world's diamonds originate in Africa, principally in Angola, Botswana, Congo, Namibia and South Africa, with the remainder coming from Russia, Canada and Australia. However, the major markets for diamonds are geographically very distant from their source, with the principle markets being traditionally the US, Japan and Italy and with new emerging markets in China, India and the Gulf States of the Middle East. Thirty per cent of the natural diamonds that are mined are gem quality and destined for use in jewellery business and 70 per cent of diamonds extracted are for industrial use (King, 2015).

The diamond supply chain for gem quality stones destined for the jewellery business is made up of the successive processes of exploration, extraction, various stages of processing and retail. We have already seen how the geographical locations of the source and the markets for diamonds impose certain constraints on the supply chain for these items. Additionally, the processing of diamonds, a highly specialized set of skills and procedures, are highly concentrated and localized in a few specific locations in the world, most notably in Antwerp, Belgium and in Johannesburg, South Africa. Indeed, Antwerp has developed a hub of expertise in its diamond quarter beginning in the 17th and 18th centuries and accelerating particularly in the 20th century when Antwerp eclipsed both Amsterdam and London as centres for the diamond trade to an extent whereby today over 80 per cent of the diamonds mined in the world now pass through Antwerp. Antwerp is now a cluster of expertise with many companies and businesses specialized in cutting and polishing diamonds, as well as being a centre for the specific financial expertise and educational centres for the business.

A further complicating factor for the diamond supply chain is that many of the locations where diamonds are mined are in areas of the world subject to extreme political instability and armed conflict. Consequently, there is a system of certification known as the Kimberley Process in place, which is a UN-mandated system of which over 70 countries are members that certifies that rough diamonds do not originate from conflict zones. Only countries that are members of the Kimberley Process may import and export rough diamonds. This certification and assurance of conflict-free origin is then further extended through the System of Warranties for polished diamonds all the way to the diamond jewellery retailer.

The diamond supply chain is therefore a system that is very much shaped by environmental, historical and security considerations. These impose many constraints on the configuration of the supply chain. They ensure that it remains relatively stable in comparison to other supply chains that are purposefully designed based on evolving business strategies and can change in response to economic and geo-political factors.

Take, for example, the supply chain of the iPhone. The iPhone is designed by Apple in California, USA. The supply of parts and components is sourced from over 30 countries around the world, including the US, China, Taiwan, Italy, South Korea, Japan, Germany, Ireland and many more. Some of the companies that supply parts for the Apple iPhone include the likes of Micron, Texas Instruments, Samsung, Murati and Infineon, to name but a few. Parts are the shipped from all over the world to assembly locations, mainly to Foxconn, a Taiwanese manufacturer, which undertakes iPhone assembly in Shenzhen and other locations in China. Assembly now takes place in Brazil also. As new models of iPhone are developed, there are continual requirements for innovation and new parts, new suppliers and new locations to be built into the supply chain. For example, one of the key challenges in the November 2018 launch of the latest iPhone models was to secure the required supply of 3D sensors for the face recognition feature of the devices. The requirements for continuous innovation, combined with cost, quality and volume capacity requirements, are paramount as the company moves towards product launch and volume supply to meet demand post launch. This is a dynamic and ever-changing supply chain challenge, which, while it presents many choices and options to the lead company Apple in terms of how, where and when it sources its components, requires very careful design and balance to meet the demands of the market.

The governance, control and management challenges presented by these contrasting supply chains are very different. Whereas in the iPhone supply chain, Apple, as the lead player to which all other suppliers and service providers are ultimately accountable, lends itself to purposeful design, control and measurement despite its geographic dispersion and the rapidity and frequency with which its configuration is changed in response to the requirements of innovation, capacity and quality requirements, the supply chain for diamonds, while it does have some dominant lead players such as De Beers, Rio Tinto and Alrosa, these cannot reconfigure their sourcing requirements in the same way. Indeed, there are fewer than 40 actively productive diamond mines in the world and the lead companies have fixed sources of supply in specific mines in specific locations in the world, for example De Beers predominantly in southern Africa, Rio Tinto in Western Australia, Zimbabwe and Northern Canada, and indeed, the Russian diamond company Alrosa which is very reliant on diamonds mined from the Verkhne-Munskoye diamond field in Siberia.

The importance of measurement

The importance of measurement is that it provides focus and clarity because what is measured becomes a focus for attention and for action. At the most basic level, one of the most powerful aids to achieving a goal is to have a metric that can be readily tracked and that indicates progress towards that goal. We all have goals in life, which may be progression in our career, achieving a certain level of savings, or maintaining a healthy weight. Without effective measurement we don't know at any given moment how we are doing and whether we are getting closer to our goal or moving away from it. Consequently, without an appropriate metric and without an effective way to measure, it is easy to lose focus, get off track or simply forget and give up on our goal altogether. Recently, I received a Fitbit as a birthday present. This is a device that you wear on your wrist like a watch, which measures your heart rate as well as your physical position. From these inputs, the device can compute your physical activity levels, how far you have moved both horizontally and vertically, the type and intensity of exercise that you do, the calories expended, your underlying resting heart rate, your cardio fitness, the number of hours slept and how that sleep breaks down in terms of deep sleep, light sleep and REM sleep. You can set health and fitness goals and track your progress over time using the device. For some of course all of this may be way too much information, but for me the device certainly helps to bring clarity and focus to the amount and frequency of the exercise that I take and its effect on some key health indicators in a simple and effective way. Indeed, the Fitbit helps illustrate several interesting aspects of measurement that can be applied to measurement in general.

Firstly, and most importantly, the things that we measure must be relevant and appropriate to the goal that we are trying to achieve. Secondly, the Fitbit simplifies and automates the collection of the data and the computation of the metrics and finally, the Fitbit presents the results in an easily understandable and impactful way quickly and effectively. Let's take each one of these points in turn and delve a little deeper.

The most important aspect of measurement is that what is being measured must be relevant and appropriate to the goal that we are trying to achieve and must clearly indicate progress towards that goal. For example, with the Fitbit if you want to ensure that you are rested and energized you can measure the duration and quality of your sleep and if you want to determine your progress towards a certain level of fitness you can measure the maximum amount of oxygen your body can use during exercise, which is called VO2 max. These metrics bear a strong relationship to, and are a clear indicator of, progress towards goals that you have deemed to be relevant and important. This seems obvious, but it is surprising how frequently inappropriate measures and metrics are used in business relation-ships between supply chain partners that bear little relevance to the desired business objectives and outcomes. Too often time and effort are wasted in the collection and computation of these metrics, only for them to be at best ignored, or at worst used as prompts for actions that do not take the business any closer to its true objectives.

In one case, I worked on helping a manufacturing company and a logistics service provider that provided warehousing and distribution transport services to the manufacturer to broaden and deepen their collaboration and to negotiate a new working relationship. When reviewing the arrangements that were current at the time, the con-tract stimulated a multitude of indicators that the service provider was required to facilitate to the client in periodic reports. Many of the indicators were irrelevant, others were ambiguous in their mean-ing and while some were actually good indicators of operational performance, there were so many and their presentation was so com-plex; they had never been used as an active management tool to ensure that the relationship was delivering the expected outcomes for each party, nor did they function as the basis for open and frank mutual discussions about achieving mutually beneficial improve-ments in the working relationships.

For the new arrangement, we had the parties think through very carefully what the most relevant and meaningful business outcomes were for the working relationship; we limited these to four or five key outcomes related to operational performance, service, quality and continuous improvement. Then we had them define very carefully what data would be required, how the metric would be computed, how frequently the results would be presented and how each metric would be used as an active management tool to drive desired actions and behaviours for the benefit of both organizations. In this way, they reduced the time and effort required to generate the key performance indicators while at the same time achieving a much better outcome in terms of the usefulness and practicality of the metrics.

The second aspect the Fitbit addresses so elegantly is that of the automated collection of the data and the computation of the metrics. Today, businesses are awash with data that resides in the databases of enterprise resource planning (ERP) systems, warehouse management systems (WMS), transport management systems (TMS) and many other applications. These raw data are a resource that only become valuable when they are processed in ways to provide inside into those aspects of performance that are of interest and that indicate progress towards specific business goals. Therefore, at this point in the process it is important to involve the company's information technology specialists so that they can determine which data are required, where those data reside, how they can be accessed and whether special applications and scripts will be required to compute the desired metrics. In some cases, there will be standard reports and metrics that the systems produce as a matter of course that may be useful, whereas in other cases it may require an investment in time and money to have the customized applications developed to produce the metrics that will be truly valuable.

The final thing that the Fitbit does well is that it presents the computed metrics in a timely and easily understandable manner, so that they can be accessed readily and used to guide and tweak behaviour on an ongoing basis to ensure that the user stays on track and makes continuous progress towards the goals that they have set for themselves. This is done through an interface on the device itself that provides real-time updates of heart rate, calories burnt, distance covered. There is also an app that can be viewed on any smart device that provides a full customizable dashboard of the metrics in real time as well as access to logs of past performance. Likewise, today in warehouse and transport operations, we see the increasing use of smart technology and applications that can present key metrics on relevant performance to operators and users in real time. For example, in warehouse operations, many providers of materials handling equipment such as fork lift trucks can fit displays based on smart technology inside the driver's cab to provide ready and easy access to dashboards of metrics relevant to the work that they are doing, such as resource utilization, jobs completed, pallet moves completed per unit time and any other metric that can be computed with the data available through the system's interfaces.

This kind of sophisticated approach to measurement has a very noticeable psychological effect on people both in operational roles and in management roles in that it appears to generate a laser-like focus and clarity on the metrics being used, particularly if they are related directly to performance assessment and reward. Therefore, the use and application of metrics and measurement in this manner needs to be approached with extreme care. There have been reports of certain organizations in the logistics space operating large distribution centres in the electronic commerce sector where metrics have been used to continuously monitor and in some cases to put pressure on workers to maintain or exceed levels of productivity that have led to burn out, disciplinary problems and industrial relations disputes. I am not advocating that approach to the use of measurement and metrics in the supply chain space. In order to generate sustainable business improvement, metrics and measures must be judiciously chosen and appropriately applied to provide focus on clarity on those aspects of business performance where they can generate a common understanding between managers and operators on the key components and actions that affect performance and provide a basis for informed and fact-based dialogue leading to continuous improvement over time in a way that is sustainable.

Measurements systems and benchmarking performance

In supply chain management and logistics operations there are several measurement frameworks that have been developed and made available to practitioners and operators that can be useful depending on what the measurement challenge and objective is. For example, the challenge of determining the productivity, quality and service levels of a single regional distribution centre is a very different challenge from that of trying to measure the effectiveness of a supply chain strategy leveraging global arbitrage opportunities and carrying on different activities of sourcing, production, and distribution of materials and products over international borders. For example, the sourcing raw materials in Australia, Russia and Brazil, manufacturing of intermediate products in China and Taiwan for transport to finishing and localization activities in Eastern Europe and Mexico, and finally on to distribution centres in North America and Western Europe for delivery to retail outlets and consumers. The measurement of the performance of a system of this nature, which involves inputs and activities from many independent stakeholders and supply chain partners, is a challenge of a very different order of scale.

Some useful measurement frameworks that are available include the following:

- *The Warehouse and Fulfilment Process Benchmark and Best Practices Guide*, which is produced by the Warehouse Education and research Council (WERC) in conjunction with the consultancy practice Supply Chain Visions (WERC & Supply Chain Visions, 2007).

- The Supply Chain Management Process Standards produced by the Council of Supply Chain Management Professionals (CSCMP & Supply Chain Visions, 2009).

- The Supply Chain Operations Reference Model (SCOR) produced by the Supply Chain Council (since 2014 merged with APICS) (APICS, 2018).

WERC Warehouse and Fulfilment Process Benchmark

The Warehouse and Fulfilment Process Benchmark and Best Practice Guide can be used as a form of workbook to pinpoint operational strengths and weaknesses in warehouse and distribution centres across a complete range of typical warehouse operating processes. These include:

- receiving and inspection;
- material handling and putaway;
- slotting;
- storage and inventory control;
- picking and packing;
- load consolidation and shipping;
- shipment documentation; and
- warehouse management system (WMS).

The way the benchmark is structured is that it breaks performance levels into five separate categories: poor practice, inadequate practice, common practice, good practice and best practice. Managers can self-assess their operation's performance into the various categories of practice based on an evaluation of the current performance levels of their operations against the process descriptions. Each of the major processes is broken down into several subprocesses that can be scored individually. For example, the receiving and inspection process is broken down into nine subcategories:

1 dock management

2 transactions

3 product labelling

4 advance shipping notice and supplier communication

5 process

6 inspection

7 cross docking

8 metrics

9 RFID

Each subprocess can be assessed and scored individually. The total of the scored can then be used to determine the overall ranking for the Receiving and Inspection Process. In the same way each of the other seven processes are broken down into their component subprocesses. In total, the eight overarching processes are subdivided into a total of almost 50 subprocesses, providing a comprehensive insight into process strengths and weaknesses that is very valuable in helping to prioritize improvement efforts to those areas that will improve performance on those elements of performance that are most critical to the strategic goals of the business. Additionally, the guide provides quantitative key performance metrics for each of process areas and breaks the score ranges out into the five categorizations of practice – poor, inadequate, common, good and best. The cut-off between the categorizations corresponds to the 20th, 40th, 60th and 80th percentile of the surveyed demographic in each case. Very usefully also, each key performance metric is clearly defined, and the data required for its calculation is specified. For example, in the Receiving and Inspection process two key performance metrics are stipulated, On Time Receipts and Perfect Order Index. The Perfect Order index is defined as 'an order that meets all of the following criteria: complete, on-time (as defined by the customer – could be on time delivery or on time shipment), perfect documentation, perfect condition' (WERC & Supply Chain Visions, 2007). The calculation of this metric is then defined as '% of on time orders multiplied by % of damage free orders multiplied by % or orders with accurate documentation as defined by the customer (e.g. invoice, ASN, labels)'. On this Perfect Order Index, Common Practice is classed as a score between 95 and 98 per cent while Best Practice requires a score greater than 99.48 per cent.

The key performance metrics set out in the original publication provide generic categorizations based on a generalized demographic at that time. However, WERC continues to produce and publish on an annual basis a DC Measures report that provides updated quantitative benchmarks for these key performance metrics and that also breaks out the metrics for key sub-groups within the demographic to provide more granular insight for specific industry sectors and operation types.

Several dozen quantitative metrics are produced, which cover the following categories:

- customer metrics
- operations metrics – inbound
- operations metrics – outbound
- financial metrics
- capacity/quality metrics
- employee metrics
- cash-to-cash metrics.

According to the DC Measures publication the most commonly used metrics in warehouse and distribution centre operations are the following:

- on-time shipments
- internal order cycle time in hours

- dock-to-stock cycle time in hours
- total order cycle time in hours
- order picking accuracy per cent by order
- average warehouse capacity used
- peak warehouse capacity used
- backorders as a per cent of total orders
- backorders as a per cent of total lines
- per cent of supplier orders received damage free
- lines picked and shipped per person hour
- lines received and put away per hour.

It is interesting to note that three of the top four metrics in use are customer-focused metrics, as are five of the top 12. In recent years there has been a tendency towards an increased focus on customer-specific measurements as companies become more aware of the importance of these metrics to positive business outcomes in sales, growth and market share, together with advances in technology that are facilitating the automation of the date capture and computation associated with these metrics.

CSCMP Supply Chain Management Process Standards

The CSCMP's Supply Chain Process Standards is a set of process standards developed for use in end-to-end supply chain operations and based on the fundamental principle that 'improvement in performance measurement is driven in large part by improved processes' (CSCMP & Supply Chain Visions, 2009). This is a very important point in the sense that the introduction of a measurement regime to track certain metrics will not of itself produce sustained improvements in performance. To move the dial significantly in this regard requires an understanding of the structure and content of the actual work processes and improvements to be made that streamline processes, reducing or eliminating non-value-added activities and many practical changes in the physical work space through the positioning of resources and consumables, enhanced technology improved training and so on, which later show up as noticeable improvements in the metrics that are being tracked.

This set of standards is broader in application than the set of WERC process benchmark and best practices discussed in the previous section. Whereas the WERC warehousing and fulfilment benchmark focuses on the performance of individual warehouses and distribution centres within businesses, the CSCMP Process Standards look at higher level supply chain processes across an entire business, of which warehousing and fulfilment are just one component. The CSCMP Process Standards take within scope five key operating processes as well as seven management and support services, as follows:

Operating processes

1 Develop vision and strategy
2 Develop and manage product and services
3 Market and sell products and services
4 Deliver products and services
5 Manage customer service.

Management and support services

1 Develop and manage human capital
2 Manage information technology
3 Manage financial resources
4 Acquire, construct, and manage property
5 Manage environmental health and safety
6 Manage external relationships
7 Manage knowledge, improvement, and change.

The standards themselves are based on the American Productivity and Quality Centre (APQC) Process Classification Framework^{SM} and present descriptive definitions for minimum and best practice attributes for process activities within process groups under the 12 categories listed above.

Across the 12 categories there are in the region of 170 different business activities related to business for which attributes are defined. Of course, not all businesses will undertake all tasks and detailed instructions are provided within the standards on how to use and apply to those activities, selectively choosing those that are relevant to each individual business situation. Two additional elements of these standards that are very useful and powerful are firstly the stress on the importance of prioritization and secondly the ability to benchmark not just qualitatively but also quantitatively across industry by reference to widely recognized cross-industry standards.

In terms of prioritization, once an assessment has been carried out of the performance of the business in relation to the processes that are relevant to its activities it is important to determine which of these are strategically important to the achievement of the strategic goals of the business so that the available resources can be applied in a prioritized manner to improvement in those areas that are going to have the greatest impact on moving the business towards the achievement of its strategic objectives.

In terms of the quantitative assessment made possible by application of the CSCMP supply chain standards the standards have been aligned with the American Productivity and Quality Centre (APQC) Process Classification Framework^{SM}. This allows companies to access independent, cross-industry benchmarks metrics that have been compiled confidentially using the inputs of thousands of participants all over the world across their business sector through the APQC's Open Standards Benchmarking Collaborative^{SM}. Participation in the survey is free and confidential.

In the supply-chain space the APQC knowledge base provides access to performance metrics across areas such as supply chain planning, procurement, manufacturing, logistics and product development.

The Supply Chain Operations Model

The Supply Chain Operations Reference (SCOR) Model, produced and endorsed by the Supply Chain Council and originally developed in 1996 (APICS, 2018) by the management consultancy PRTM, now part of PwC, is a comprehensive Supply Chain framework used to describe, measure and evaluate supply chains as well as providing a framework and model for the strategic design of end-to-end supply chains.

The SCOR model is based around four major pillars across six distinct management processes.

The four pillars are:

1 process modelling and re-engineering

2 performance measures

3 best practices

4 skills.

The six management processes that are covered are:

1 plan

2 source

3 make

4 deliver

5 return

6 enable.

Each one of these high-level management process is further broken down into three levels of process detail. Level 1 defines the elements of scope such as the context, geographies, market segments and products. Level 2 defines the configuration of the supply chain within the elements of the scope; for example, within Level 2 of the Make process there are the possible configurations of:

- make build to stock;
- make build to order; and
- make engineer to order.

Level 3 describes the elemental detail of the processes and their performance attributes and identifies the key business activities within the configuration.

The usefulness and the power of adopting a recognized and standardized model and framework for describing, measuring and evaluating the supply chain as well as to design and configure the supply chain is that these models can enable effective communication among supply chain partners by providing a common understanding of concepts, vocabulary and activities. Additionally, they can be used to benchmark performance against peer groups and cohorts and contribute to the both internal and external recognition of performance levels, trends and achievements. Furthermore, such models provide a very useful framework for the evaluation of alternative supply chain configurations, whether for the purposes of ongoing continuous improvement or for strategy formulation.

Summary

In this chapter we have discussed how measurement in a supply chain context presents us with some special challenges due to the nature of modern-day supply chains, involving as they invariably do, multiple independent supply chain partners who often participate in many different supply chains in which they have different roles, responsibilities and accountabilities.

We have also seen how different supply chains operate under very different constraints and dynamics that present very diverse measurement challenges and we discussed two very contrasting supply chains, that for the exploration, extraction and processing of diamonds for the retail jewellery sector with that of Apple's iPhone. The former is a supply chain dominated by several environmental, geographical and administrative constraints of long duration contrasted with the more dynamic and fluctuating global supply chain of the Apple supply chain that is continually renewed and reconfigured in response to the challenges of innovation, quality and volume capacity.

We have highlighted the crucial importance of measurement in the supply chain because effective measurement brings focus and clarity to what is important in moving the business, and the collaborative relationships of which the business is composed, towards predefined strategic business goals as well as providing a common understanding among supply chain participants regarding what is happening, what needs to be done and what will be the effects of certain courses of action.

We have presented several recognized supply chain measurement and benchmarking frameworks that are in use. The first of these was the more single-facility focused Warehouse and Fulfilment Process Benchmark produced by the Warehouse Education and Research Council (WERC), which provides process standards for the main operational processes that take place within one key component of the supply chain – the warehouse and distribution centre, as well as being linked to the annual DC Measures publication from WERC that sets out the industry benchmarks for a long list of metrics that are compiled from a wide demographic of industry sectors and types of operations.

The next operational measurement framework that we examined was the more end-to-end Supply Chain Management Process Standards produced by the Council of Supply Chain Management Professionals (CSCMP & Supply Chain Visions, 2009). This framework encourages operators to move on from an exclusive focus on metrics to one of process improvement in the fundamental belief that performance improvement against key metrics can only be achieved from actions taken to streamline and improve the underlying work processes. This framework looks at higher-level supply chain processes than the WERC framework across an entire business. Indeed, the CSCMP Process Standards take within scope five key operating processes including strategy, operations and customer service as well as seven management and support services including technology, human capital and finance. Very usefully also, the CSCMP Supply Chain Management Process standards are aligned to the American Productivity and Quality Centre (APQC) Process Classification Framework[SM]. This allows companies to access independent, cross-industry benchmarks metrics that have been compiled using the inputs of thousands of participants all over the world across multiple business sectors through the APQC's Open Standards Benchmarking Collaborative[SM], participation in which is free and confidential.

The last measurement framework that we examined was the Supply Chain Operations Reference Model (SCOR) produced by the Supply Chain Council (APICS, 2018), which has been merged with APICS since 2014. The SCOR model is used to describe, measure and evaluate supply chains as well as providing a framework and model for the strategic design of end-to-end supply chains based on a comprehensive structure around the four pillars of process improvement, metrics, best practices and skills across the six-key supply chain management processes of plan, source, make, deliver, return and enable.

This standardized model and framework for describing, measuring and evaluating the supply chain as well as to design and configure the supply chain enables effective communication among supply chain partners by providing a common understanding of concepts, vocabulary and activities. Additionally, it can be used to benchmark performance against peer groups and contribute to recognition of performance levels, trends and goal achievements, as well as providing a very useful framework for the evaluation of alternative supply chain configurations for ongoing continuous improvement and for strategy formulation.

All these measurement and benchmarking frameworks may have a role to play in your business measurement endeavours to help you keep your finger on the pulse. Indeed, depending on the scope of the area or system of interest all can be applicable and useful. However, the single most important thing to remember regarding supply chain measurement is that we measure what is important and that what is important is what we measure.

References

APICS (2018) SCOR Supply Operations Reference Model. Available from: www.apics.org/apics-for-business/frameworks/scor [last accessed 1 June 2018]

CSCMP & Supply Chain Visions Ltd (2009) Supply Chain Management Process Standards, The Council of Supply Chain Management Professionals (CSCMP), Lombard, IL

King, Herbert M (2015) Which Countries Produce the Most Gem
Diamonds. Available from: https://geology.com/articles/gem-diamond-
map/ [last accessed 17 May 2018]

WERC & Supply Chain Visions Ltd (2007) *The Warehousing and
Fulfillment Process Benchmark & Best Practices Guide*, Warehouse
Education and Research Council, Oak Brook, IL

Looking around the block 10
Future trends

Predicting the future is always a risky business. Nonetheless, many of the megatrends in technology, demographics and the environment are structural and clearly visible in today's world. These will continue to exert their influence and shape the future landscape in which businesses will need to learn to operate, innovate and thrive. Additionally, what is already happening in some parts of the world and sectors of business will likely come to pass in others. It is good to be prepared and to avoid being caught unawares by the changes and innovations that will shape the supply chain configurations of tomorrow. Geopolitical developments such as Brexit and growing US trade protectionism mean that businesses that operate internationally, rather than throwing in the towel and falling back exclusively on home-based markets, will continue to look for new and innovative supply chain solutions to mitigate the effects of obstacles such as tariffs and other non-tariff trade barriers. As Professor Pankaj Ghemawat of IESE business school in Barcelona points out in much of his writing, the process of business globalization is at best only a partial and very uneven process, with most interactions and flows still taking place within countries and among nearby neighbours and consequently there is still considerable scope for the further broadening and deepening of international trading relations and flows particularly within regional blocs (Ghemawat, 2011). In this chapter we are going to round out our considerations of the importance of international supply chain relationships by looking forward in time with a mixture of extrapolation and speculation regarding some of the major trends that we see in the world today that, I believe, will have significant impacts on the future of international supply chain relationships. To do this we will look at five separate but interrelated trends that I believe will be among the most influential in shaping the supply chains of the future:

1 The increased deployment of automation and robotics;

2 The further integration of information and communications technologies;

3 The increase in international trade and the proliferation of international free trade agreements;

4 The wider participation of smaller and medium-sized enterprises in international business; and

5 Innovative solutions for the delivery of capacity and infrastructure to businesses.

We will take each in turn and examine the current state situation and attempt to cast our view forward over the next 10 or 20 years.

Automation and robotics

My prediction is that a combination of technological advances, demographic pressure and labour shortages will see the ever-increasing deployment of automation and robotics solutions in logistics and supply chain activities such as transport, warehousing and distribution. In May of 2018, the US unemployment rate dropped to 3.9 per cent per cent and continued its downward trajectory (Bureau of Labor Statistics, 2018). This was the lowest reported figure for US unemployment since 2000. Likewise, in the United Kingdom, the unemployment rate had dropped to 4.2 per cent, in early 2018, while in Japan it was 2.5 per cent and even in the Euro Area (EA19) where unemployment had been stubbornly high for over a decade in the wake of the great recession, the financial and the euro crisis, the unemployment rate in early 2018 had fallen to its lowest level since 2008, reaching 8.5 per cent over the entire 19-country currency bloc and in some of its core economies it had fallen to record low levels such as in Germany at 3.4 per cent and in the Netherlands to 3.9 per cent. In a parallel megatrend, the demographic profile of these developed economies in North America, Europe and Asia has been shifting in recent decades to one in which population growth is stagnating and older people are becoming an increasingly large proportion of the population due to a combination of increased longevity and lower fertility rates. This means that the total populations of most developed countries, in the absence of substantial and sustained immigration, may begin to decline. For example, in most developed countries, the population replacement fertility rate is about 2.1 births per woman. The fertility rate in most developed economies, and in some developing countries such as China, is currently well below the replacement rate. For example, the fertility rate in the US is 1.87, in Germany it is 1.45, in Japan 1.41 and in China 1.6 (CIA, 2018). Consequently, to continue to grow their economies in the face of aging and stagnating populations, these countries will have to extend the working age, increase immigration and increase productivity per worker. All these measures can lead to social tensions and push back in one form or another and each country will adopt a mix of these measures that suit its individual set of circumstances, challenges and political realities.

One way in which countries can increase productivity per worker is with the automation of tasks and jobs through the application of robotics and other enhanced automation technologies such as artificial intelligence and the internet of things. The sector in which the deployment of robotics has advanced most in recent decades is in manufacturing. According to the International Federation of Robotics, the robot density in manufacturing, defined as the number of robots deployed per 10,000 workers increased worldwide from 66 in 2015 to 74 in 2016 (IFR, 2018). In those countries where the deployment of robots has advanced most, namely South Korea, Singapore, Germany and Japan, the robot density in manufacturing has already exceeded 300 per 10,000. Table 10.1 indicates the robot density per 10,000 manufacturing workers in the 10 most automated countries in the world. Many of these countries, such as Singapore, Taiwan, South Korea, Germany and Italy, are also among those with the lowest fertility rates in the world.

Table 10.1   Robot density versus fertility by country

Ranking	Country	Mfg Robot Density per 10,000 Workers	Fertility Rate (Births per Woman)
1	South Korea	631	1.26
2	Singapore	488	0.83
3	Germany	309	1.45
4	Japan	303	1.41
5	Sweden	223	1.88
6	Denmark	211	1.73
7	US	189	1.87
8	Italy	185	1.44
9	Belgium	184	1.78
10	Taiwan	177	1.03

The process of robot deployment in manufacturing has been going on for several decades already, particularly in the automotive industry. However, recent developments and advances in sensor technology and artificial intelligence have now paved the way for the deployment of robotics and automated systems across many other sectors with a more direct impact on the supply chain activities of companies in the distribution and logistics services sectors. Two areas of interest are in the highly labour-intensive areas of distribution-order picking and the driving of heavy goods vehicles where labour shortages are already beginning to become evident as labour markets tighten in response to the economic and demographic changes discussed earlier. For example, in the US there are approximately 8 million people who make their living as drivers and of these about 3 million are truck drivers (Alltrucking, 2018). However, in the US as in Europe and other developed economies, fewer and fewer young people are entering the profession, even as the numbers of working age people entering the workforce continues to decline and workers retire from the sector at the end of their working lives. Consequently, several companies such as Uber and Otto have been investing heavily in research and development in the field of self-driving freight trucks. Indeed, Uber is providing self-driving trucking services in Arizona in the US and has reportedly completed over 2 million driven miles by self-driving freight trucks (Della Cava, 2018). Currently, these trucks are not advanced enough for full dock-to-dock runs and are limited to highway runs between hubs with a safety driver on board. The pick-ups and drop-offs are still done in the conventional manner with a human driver. There are many technological, administrative and social hurdles to overcome before self-driving vehicles replace human drivers completely and the process may take many years; nonetheless the economic and demographic factors that are present coupled with the technological advances that have already been made indicate that this is a sure sign of things to come.

Switching from outside to inside the large logistics hubs and distribution centres that are significant components of modern supply chains; for many years now automated systems have been deployed for the automated storage and retrieval of goods for presentation to human order pickers using enhancements such as pick by light, voice picking and pick by vision technology. These types of solutions have been particularly common in large distribution centres for food, pharma, fashion and media but the last step of item selection for order picking has continued to depend on teams of human order pickers.

In recent years, however, advances in robotics, particularly in the sensitivity and precision of sensor technology, as well as in artificial intelligence, has enabled robotics to break into this last redoubt of manual work. Again, as in the case with self-driving vehicles, the human element is not eliminated completely, but the role, as well as the knowledge, and skills required of the human actors, are changing radically even as the number of human operators decreases. One good example is that of the autonomous mobile robots developed originally by Kiva Systems, now Amazon Robotics, and deployed extensively by Amazon in their distribution centres around the world. The number of robots now operated by Amazon worldwide exceeds 100,000 (Wingfield, 2017). Perhaps surprisingly, as Amazon has grown and deployed more and more robots its human workforce has also increased dramatically, but the type of work that its warehouse operatives now perform has changed with less walking and lifting and more supervision and trouble-shooting of the automated systems.

In the Amazon warehouses, armies of autonomous mobile robots coordinated by sophisticated software systems move entire shelving units that contain the inventory required for the fulfilment of customers' orders to pick stations manned by human operatives who complete the last step which involves manually picking the required items into the order boxes. Notwithstanding the large increases in the workforce at Amazon, the number of human warehouse workers required is far less than what it would have been required without the deployment of the robots, though it is debatable whether the company would even have been able to expand operations at such a pace without the robot deployment. This illustrates that the connection between the increase in the numbers of robots and the decrease in the number of human jobs is not quite as straightforward as it might appear at first sight. Indeed, Amazon has added some 80,000 people to its workforce since its acquisition of the Kiva technology, bringing the total to about 125,000 (Wingfield, 2017).

Integration of information and communications technologies

My prediction is that the integration of communications and information processing technologies, together with wireless and mobile technologies, the internet of things and big data processing will enable dramatic improvements in efficiencies, economic opportunities and service offerings in the fields of global sourcing, manufacturing, distribution and resource optimization that are still impractical and cost prohibitive today. Over the last 30 years or so, a digital revolution has unfolded, initially with the arrival of main frame and later personal computing and the deployment of information processing systems across many businesses. However, up until quite recently, all these information processing systems were standalone without integration links between producers, processors and consumers. Enterprise Resource Planning (ERP), Warehouse Management Systems (WMS), Transport Management Systems (TMS) and many of the other applications all existed and operated independently and in isolation from each other. In more recent years we have seen the emergence and rapid advance of wireless and mobile technology coupled with a huge increase in the capacity to store and analyse data. This has enabled many different systems to be integrated across multiple physical locations and across corporate boundaries. Notwithstanding, the real and ongoing technological challenges involved in guaranteeing the integrity, safety and security of data, these advances have brought us to the cusp of a revolution in integrated data solutions that promises to enable organizations to collect and analyse data for everything from the best setting for machine tools to the optimum number of distribution vehicles to operate, to which colours and product designs are the most desirable for their customers.

Simultaneously, we are seeing the emergence of the internet of things (IoT), whereby everyday objects are embedded with IoT devices that collect and send data about their condition, position and status on a continuous basis. This data, coupled with enhanced analytics capabilities is providing heretofore unparalleled insight and opportunities for optimization in fields such as precision agriculture, healthcare, and waste management among others. Together with blockchain technology, these solutions will greatly enhance the integrity and security of supply chains, particularly those in which authentication, traceability and temperature control are of paramount importance. One interesting example is that provided by Big Belly Smart City Solutions, a Massachusetts-based company that originally developed a solar-powered, compacting street rubbish-bin solution for use in public places.

The solar-powered big-belly bin was installed in Colorado in 2014 and since then, has been deployed across the US and Canada as well as in countries such as the Netherlands, the UK, Germany, Sweden, Iceland and Switzerland (Boteler, 2017). Recently, I have seen the Big Belly bins being installed in my home city, Dublin, in Ireland. These bins, which compact rubbish by a factor of five by means of a chain driven compactor powered by the bin's solar panel, are smart in the sense that they have built-in sensors that report their status remotely to the operator's central dashboard. This provides management and administration data that yield highly valuable information for the coordination of cleaning and clearing activities as well as about the behaviour, the quantity and type of rubbish generated at different kinds of locations. The company has transformed itself into a platform-type business model for the provision of smart city solutions for waste and recycling as well as the deployment of WIFI hotspots, urban sensors for footfall and noise pollution, alert beacons and first responder networks.

More smaller businesses trading internationally

My prediction is that we will see more and more small- and medium-sized enterprises all over the world leveraging international supply chain relationships to make their businesses more profitable, more resilient and more sustainable. The current US administration is concerned about out-of-kilter trade deficits with some of its key trading partners such as the EU, China and Japan. Whatever the rights and wrongs of alleged unfair trade practices, currency manipulation and unfavourable free trade agreements, an astonishing fact about American business today is that only about 1 per cent of American companies export to markets outside the US. Therefore, one very effective way for the US to redress this trade imbalance is for American companies to make more of the things that people abroad want to buy and export more of them to developed and developing economies around the world. There are great opportunities for American SMEs to expand into markets in Latin America, Canada, the European Union and East Asia if they have the desire and the vision to do so.

At this moment in time, with a relatively soft dollar, combined with most major regional economies around the world showing healthy growth, coupled with the technological advances in information processing and communications technology and the comprehensive service offerings in international transport and logistics that are available through third party and fourth party logistics service providers, this is a challenge that, notwithstanding the risks, has never been more of a practical proposition for small- and medium-sized enterprises in the US. Indeed, the US government's International Trade Administration (ITA) website states the following, 'Free Trade Agreements (FTAs) have proved to be one of the best ways to open up foreign markets to US exporters. Trade Agreements reduce barriers to US exports, and protect US interests and enhance the rule of law in the FTA partner country' (ITA, 2018). The ITA then go on to state that 47 per cent of US goods exports, worth a total of $710 billion per annum go to the 20 or so countries with which the US has standing free trade agreements. Additionally, the US maintains a trade surplus with these FTA partners that amounted to $12 billion in 2015. In addition to the NAFTA members Canada and Mexico, the countries with which the US currently has standing free trade agreements are Australia, Bahrain, Chile, Colombia, Costa Rica, Dominican Republic, El Salvador, Guatemala, Honduras, Nicaragua, Israel, Jordan, South Korea, Morocco, Oman. Panama, Peru and Singapore.

Likewise, small- and medium-sized companies in the European Union are integrating increasingly into the international supply chains crisscrossing the 28-member European Single Market and the 19-member euro currency zone as well as with markets further afield. These networks are being tapped both as sources of supply as well as markets for their own products. Indeed, in my own country Ireland, the Irish Exporters Association, in a recent survey of members, many of them small- and medium-sized exporting companies, noted that between 2016 and 2018, the proportion of companies that were looking to diversify their export markets as a mitigation for uncertainty regarding the future ease of access to UK markets post-Brexit had risen from 54 to 66 per cent. The top diversification locations being, in order of importance, Germany, US, France, Spain, Australia, Netherlands, Canada, Belgium, Italy and Sweden.

This is testament to a preference for trading with other EU partners within the immediate geographic region on the one hand and with nations further afield with which Ireland shares linguistic, cultural and administrative affiliations such as the US, Canada and Australia. This increasing intra-regional trade within the European union is borne out by the fact that the intra-EU exports of goods almost doubled between 2002 and 2008 (Eurostat, 2018), from about €150 billion to over €290 billion and this despite a crash of almost €60 billion in 2008 in the wake of the global economic crisis. In the United Kingdom in late 2016, in the aftermath of the result of the

Brexit referendum, Bibby Financial Services SME Tracker indicated that an increasing proportion of British SMEs were investing in exporting, with the proportion having risen to 15 per cent in Q3 2016 as compared to just 8 per cent a year earlier.

All of this is being driven by a combination of factors that includes the fact that competitors from developed and developing countries are accessing the markets that home-based SMEs considered reserved to themselves up until recently. Additionally, the communications and information processing technology innovations that we have discussed elsewhere have made it practical and cost-effective for SMEs to develop and maintain good working relationships with supply chain partners, whether suppliers, customers or service providers, across borders in ways that were not feasible or affordable in the past. Important also in this trend is the need to innovate, diversify and tap into new ideas, new materials, and new services to increase the competitiveness, resilience and robustness of smaller- and medium-sized companies.

Increase in international trade and free trade agreements

My prediction is that international trade volume will continue to grow steadily as countries and trading blocs will seek to implement preferential free trade agreements with myriad other countries, particularly those in their regional neighbourhood, as they seek new sources of competitive supply as well as markets for their own output. Much has been made in recent years about the UK's upcoming exit from the European Union, the European Single Market and the European Customs Union, a process known as Brexit, as well as the risk of the North America Free Trade Association (NAFTA) agreements being watered down or torn up altogether and the refusal of the US administration to ratify the Trans-Pacific Partnership (TPP) agreement in 2017. No doubt these are developments that present challenges to international trade and interregional trade. However, what lies behind some of these developments is not so much a desire to discontinue trade, but rather a wish to rebalance or reconfigure it in ways that address certain concerns that the politicians and electorates of some countries have expressed in recent years. Indeed, at the time of writing both the Brexit and NAFTA negotiations are continuing in earnest with the various parties trying to find accommodations that address their concerns while maintaining mutually beneficial trading relationships for the future. Likewise, in February 2018, the Trump administration let it be known that it might be open to considering re-engagement with the TTP partners (Domm, 2018), Australia, Brunei, Canada, Chile, Japan, Malaysia, Mexico, New Zealand, Peru, Singapore, and Vietnam, who persevered after the withdrawal of the US from the TPP and signed off on a deal called the Comprehensive and Progressive Agreement for Trans-Pacific Partnership, which embodies most of the provisions of the original TPP deal.

What has received much less attention, however, during the same period has been the ongoing international trend of forging an ever-increasing number of free trade agreements both between individual countries and between large trading blocs such as the EU, EFTA, Mercosur, and others. Some notable recent examples that are either concluded already or at various stages of negotiation include the following:

- The Pacific Alliance Free Trade Area comprised of Chile, Colombia, Mexico and Peru;
- The African Continental Free Trade Area under negotiation involving 55 African countries;
- EU individual FTAs with Canada, Mexico, South Korea, Japan and Turkey;
- China bilateral FTAs with Australia, South Korea and Switzerland;
- Japan bilateral FTAs with the EU, Australia, Mexico, India and Switzerland;
- EFTA FTAs with Mexico, Canada, South Korea and Turkey;
- India negotiations with EU and EFTA although these are currently suspended; and
- Mercosur negotiations with EU and EFTA, which have been reopened.

There are many other examples, and this trend is set to continue to open opportunities for small- and medium-sized enterprises as well as larger corporates in these countries enabling them to access additional sources of competitive supply and export opportunities. We have already seen that the US has FTAs in place with over 20 countries and the United Kingdom post-Brexit has signalled its intention to negotiate as many as 40 new free trade agreements with other countries and trading blocs around the world with top priorities being with the EU itself as well as the US, China, India, Canada, Japan and Saudi Arabia.

Notwithstanding the ebb and flow of free trade agreements on the one hand and the erection of trade and non-trade barriers due to protectionism and economic nationalism on the other, international supply chains and the relationships that tie them together are the best way to creatively and legally navigate the challenges of borders and obstacles and to take advantage of the openings and opportunities on the international business stage.

While there has been a lot of turbulence, debate and argument on the advantages and disadvantages of free trade and an apparent drift towards protectionism since 2016, international trade volumes have begun to pick up. World trade volumes posted their highest growth rate for six years in 2017 after a sharp decline in 2008 and for some time thereafter (WTO, 2017). Predictions for international trade growth in 2018 and 2019 continue to be strong. Indeed, there is some indication that the intensity of trade within geographical regions such as Europe, North America and East Asia is intensifying and growing at a faster rate than trade between these regions.

The clear message is that international trade is not going through a period of drastic retrenchment now as happened during the wave of extreme protectionism and nationalism that swept the world in the 1930s. During the 1930s, a combination of factors conspired to cause international trade to shrink by two thirds in three years (Ortiz-Espina and Roser, 2018). This is not happening now by my reading, but rather international trade is changing its patterns and flows to adapt to the new geopolitical realities that are emerging on the world stage.

Innovation in capacity and infrastructure provision

My prediction is that companies will become more creative and more competent at accessing resources based on as-needed, service-type arrangements that generate operational expenditures rather than investing their own capital to access assets, resources and services that they consider non-core such as those related to the movement, storage and manipulation of materials and products. This will be enabled and catalysed by some of the technological advances that we have already discussed and will give rise to a multiplicity of new service offerings. Many of these service offerings will be provided through platform-based business models giving access to resources such as physical assets, software, utilities and consumables in ways that are currently not yet practical or cost effective.

Since the 1980s there has been a veritable explosion in the outsourcing of business functions and activities considered as non-core by brand owners ranging from cleaning and catering to human resource management and product development. In the world of logistics and supply chain, this has led to the emergence of companies referred to as third party logistics service providers (3PL). Many companies in manufacturing and distribution have partnered with these logistics service providers at home and abroad. This has enabled them to focus on what they deem to be their core activities and strengths, whether that be research and development, manufacturing, or sales and marketing, and they have contracted out many of their requirements in warehousing, transport, freight forwarding and other value-adding logistics activities to these logistics service providers.

In more recent times, another type of logistics service provider, referred to as a fourth party logistics service provider (4PL) has emerged onto the scene. These take different forms, and many have emerged from the technology, software and consultancy arenas rather than the sector of transportation and warehousing, often informally referred to as the world of 'sheds and wheels', as has generally been the case with the traditional third-party logistics service providers.

Whereas the 3PLs generally own and operate assets such as warehouses and trucks and manage the movement, storage and handling of their clients' materials and products, 4PLs provide a higher-level supply chain management offering, whereby they take on the procurement, management, sourcing and development of complete sections of their clients supply chains without necessarily owning any assets. Whereas many 3PLs have regional of sectoral strengths, 4PLs will coordinate and manage the activities of multiple 3PLs across sectoral and regional boundaries providing just one interface for the client. Again, these are models that are set to benefit greatly from the advances in information processing and communications technologies and some will emerge as platform-type offerings akin to some of the consumer-based platform offerings that people are now familiar with such as Uber and AirBnB for commodity-type services whereas others will provide highly integrated service offerings requiring deep levels of understanding, trust and coordination with their clients.

As well as continued and more sophisticated outsourcing of functions and tasks we will see an ever-increasing array of possibilities to access and use resources and assets based on service models rather than acquisition models, with on-demand access as opposed to owning the asset or the resource that provides the service. There has already been considerable development of the software a service (SaaS) model in recent years providing access on a subscription basis to software resources for Enterprise Resource Planning (ERP) systems, Warehouse Management Systems (WMS), Transport Management Systems (TMS) and many more. Notwithstanding the data security and confidentiality challenges that need to be managed carefully, particularly with new data protection regulations such as Europe's General Data Protection Regulation (GDPR, 2018) that came into effect across the European Union on 25 May 2018, we are likely to continue to see expanding SaaS offerings.

SaaS is particularly attractive to small- and medium-sized businesses because it gives them access to high-end tools based on as-needed, readily scalable models, without the need for large capital expenditures thus giving them access to capabilities and capacities that previously were the exclusive preserve of larger companies with deep pockets. Other, less obvious, resources that will be provided as services include lighting, power, heat, data storage and many more.

One company making inroads in this space is Urban Volt, the Dublin-based provider of light as a service (LaaS ®) to commercial and industrial clients (Paul, 2016). In this model, highly energy-efficient LED lighting is fitted or retrofitted in the client's facility with no upfront outlay on the part of the client. Urban Volt makes the full capital investment for the fit out. The client uses the lighting as normal and pays Urban Volt a service charge that is less than what it would have paid the utility provider for the power consumed by its traditional lighting solution. Urban Volt makes its money by sharing in the savings in the clients' energy bill over five years. This is a solution that is proving to be particularly beneficial in warehouses, distribution centres, factories and retail outlets where high-quality lighting is required on an always-on basis. This company is now expanding operations to the US and Europe as well as into other service areas such as 'Solar as a Service', which combined with battery storage solutions will enable the provision of full energy solutions on an as-a-service basis, with the potential and indeed the stated ambition to take many of its customers off the national electricity grid altogether in the future.

Another development that we are seeing, particularly with manufacturing companies, is a reluctance to invest their own capital in logistics assets and infrastructure such as warehouse buildings, storage and materials handling equipment and the accompanying software solutions required to operate such facilities. These companies have realized that they can add more value to their own businesses by investing in core capabilities such as research and development, manufacturing technology, sales and marketing. As a result, we are seeing in our own consultancy business how many of our manufacturing and distribution sector clients are looking to outside service providers to bring innovative financial solutions to the table to develop and deliver logistics infrastructure and to provide it to the manufacturers and distributors based on long-term bundled service agreements.

Final note

In this chapter we have explored just a few of the areas relevant to supply chain management where the shape of things to come can already be seen. As I stated at the outset of the chapter, predicting the future is always a risky business, and yet it is very worthwhile to try to peer through the fog to attempt to discern where lies the potential to leverage human creativity and people's innate desire to connect, to learn and to prosper. My belief is that the development and improvement of the condition of our businesses, our communities and the wider world, will depend to a large degree on the quality of the working relationships that we build with supply chain partners at home and abroad. This will be a crucial ingredient in helping us to overcome the real challenges that we encounter and to take advantage of the real opportunities that the changes and developments underway in today's world present to us. I have no doubt that whatever does unfold in the future, the ability to envision, set up and maintain high-quality supply chain relationships, whether short term or long term, will be the key differentiator and lever of competitive advantage in the years ahead.

References

Alltrucking.com (2018) Truck Drivers in the USA. Available from www.alltrucking.com [last accessed 1 September 2018]

Boteler, C (2017) How Bigbelly is Leveraging its Compactors for Smart City Solutions (Smartcity dives 29/9) Available from www.smartcitydive.com [last accessed 5 August 2018]

Bureau of Labor Statistics (2018) Labor Force Statistics from the Current Population Survey. Available from www.data.bls.gov [last accessed 7 September 2018]

Central Intelligence Agency (2018) Total Fertility Rate – The World Factbook. Available from www.cia.gov [last accessed 8 August 2018]

Della Cava, M (2018) Uber Trucks Start Shuttling Goods Across Arizona – by Themselves (USA Today 6/3). Available from www.eu.usatoday.com [last accessed 27 August 2018]

Domm, P (2018) Trans-Pacific Trade Deal Could Solve a Big Problem for Trump, but it may be Difficult to Rejoin (CNBC 17/4). Available from www.cnbc.com [last accessed 5 August 2018]

Eurostat (2018) Intra-EU Trade in Goods: Recent Trends. Available from https://eu.europa.eu [last accessed 28 July 2018]

General Data Protection Regulation (2018) The EU General Data Protection Regulation (GDPR). Available from https://eugdpr.org [last accessed 10 June 2018]

Ghemawat, P (2011) *World 3.0, Global Prosperity and How to Achieve It*, Harvard Business Review Press, Boston, MA

International Federation of Robotics (2018) World Robotics, Statistics. Available from www.ifr.org [last accessed 20 August 2018]

International Trade Administration (2018) Free Trade Agreements. Available from www.trade.gov [last accessed 7 July 2018]

Ortiz-Espina, E. and Roser, M. (2018) International Trade. Available from https://ourworldindata.org/international-trade [last accessed 15 August 2018]

Paul, M (2016) Urban Volt Energised by €30m Financing Deal with Swiss Fund (*Irish Times* 1/11). Available from https://irishtimes.com [last accessed 26 June 2018]

Wingfield, N (2017) The Robots of Amazon, p B1, *New York Times,* 11 September 2017

Wingfield, N (2017) As Amazon Pushes Forward with Robots, Workers Find New Roles (*New York Times*, 10/9). Available from www.nytimes.com [last accessed 1 September 2018]

World Trade Organisation (2017) Trade Statistics – World Trade Statistical Review 2017. Available from www.wto.org [last accessed 21 July 2018]

INDEX

NB: page numbers in *italic* indicate figures or tables